HOW TO WORK
IN SOMEONE ELSE'S
COUNTRY

HOW TO WORK IN SOMEONE ELSE'S COUNTRY

RUTH STARK

UNIVERSITY OF
WASHINGTON PRESS
Seattle & London

This publication is supported in part by the Donald R. Ellegood International Publications Endowment.

UNIVERSITY OF WASHINGTON PRESS

P.O. Box 50096, Seattle, WA 98145, U.S.A.

www.washington.edu/uwpress

LIBRARY OF CONGRESS CATALOGING-IN-PUBLICATION DATA

Stark, Ruth D.

How to work in someone else's country / Ruth D. Stark. — 1st ed.

    p. cm.

Includes bibliographical references and index.

ISBN 978-0-295-99136-8 (pbk. : alk. paper)

1. Foreign workers—Developing countries.

2. Interpersonal relations—Developing countries.

3. Developing countries—Social life and customs.

I. Title.

HD6300.S736 2011   650.1091724—dc23   2011017793

And I have made a mistake, Robert Jordan thought to himself. I have told Spaniards we can do something better than they can when the rule is never to speak of your own exploits or abilities. . . . I have told them what I think they should do and now they are furious.

—Ernest Hemingway, *For Whom the Bell Tolls*

CONTENTS

FOREWORD

BY BILL BICKNELL, MD, MPH

This down-to-earth and practical guide emphasizes what many of us overlook or forget. Working overseas is first and foremost about relationships, respect, and the ability to listen and learn. This sounds simple and obvious, but it is not. Technical skills are important, but they are no more than a beginning and are never sufficient alone. Dr. Stark gives examples of what to do, what not to do, and why. She provides a reader-friendly guide packed with pearls of wisdom. Whether you are about to embark on your first overseas assignment or have been in the business for years, you will find much here of value and relevance. I did.

Although written from a health perspective, the principles and approaches suggested are applicable in any field. A paragraph from the last chapter merits quoting:

> *When you are working abroad, your greatest tool is yourself—your sincerity, your caring, your wisdom, and your sensitivity. In the end, being successful on a job overseas depends as much on who you are as it does on what you do.*

A key theme is the importance of respect: Respect for individuals, for organizations, for cultures, and for nations. My own experience suggests that the most serious, common, and glaring mistakes we make as expatriates are to forget we are guests, forget to listen, forget we can learn, forget we do not have all the answers, and forget that arrogance makes enemies.

A simple rule is the one many of our mothers taught us: "Do unto others as you would have them do unto you." If we listened and looked at ourselves honestly, would we accept our behavior if we were on the receiving end of it? Often, the honest answer is a resounding no! Dr. Stark helps us understand why this is the case. She suggests ways to suffer less disappointment overseas and shows us how to be more effective and do a far better job with more enjoyment and more satisfaction.

If you are early in your career or if this is your first trip abroad, every chapter counts. However, I have known experienced consultants who should have known better and would benefit from every chapter. If you are more experienced, you may want to skip over the travel tips and dress code.

Readable, relevant, and *very helpful* are terms that sum up this book. Read it on the plane, or better yet, read it before you pack and before your final plans are made. I will use this in teaching professionals as they begin their international careers and will recommend it to all who work abroad.

This is truly a practical guide for students and professionals, and it will help you learn how to be successful when you work in someone else's country. Tuck this book into your carry-on bag and share it with friends and colleagues. You won't regret it.

Bill Bicknell, MD, MPH
Professor of International Health, Family Medicine, and Socio-Medical Sciences
Founding Chairman, Department of International Health
Boston University

A NOTE TO THE READER

This is the book I have been threatening to write for over twenty years.

Every time I sent an international worker off to a distant land and every time one of those well-meaning workers blew it, I told myself that I must write this book. But I never got down to the task.

Then my daughter got an international job, and I decided that the time had come to put pen to paper and to share with her the lessons I had learned over my many years of working overseas. Like every parent, I wanted my daughter to be successful and to avoid the blunders that can make an international assignment turn sour.

So I gathered up the journal notes I had written over the years—mostly on scraps of paper and on the backs of envelopes—and shared them with her. As we exchanged "stories from the field," I became convinced that, although we are in different professions (she in finance and I in health), the "dos and don'ts" of international work were much the same, whatever the profession and wherever the country.

There are many textbooks on consulting. This is not one of them. There are no references to academic or professional journals here. Rather, this book is my attempt to share with you the practical lessons I have learned over more than three decades working as an international professional in Latin America, Asia, Africa, and the Pacific Islands.

ACKNOWLEDGMENTS

Many friends and colleagues have reviewed this book, added points, and contributed examples and "stories from the field." I am deeply grateful for their contributions and for their encouragement. My special thanks to Sandra Anderson, Jan Atwood, Richard Bauer, Bill Bicknell, Bob Burke, Jaco Cilliers, Peter Clark, Davor Dakovic, Debbie DeVoe, John Donahue, Ann Downer, Lois Elred, Virginia Fowkes, Merla Garrett, Janet Glover, F. Gray Handley, Bob Jud, Karen Kelley, Silke Mallmann, Theresa Miller, Joan Mumaw, Alison Munro, Janet Quillian, Elizabeth Reid, Joyce Smith, Dave Snyder, Stephen Stark, Taryn Stark, Patricia Vanderburg, and Joel Vanderburg.

To all my professional colleagues and friends in the countries where I have worked, I thank you for sharing your wisdom and enriching my life.

To my daughter, Taryn, I dedicate this book to you as you embark on your exciting venture. My wish for you is that your life journey will be filled with the richness of experience that I have enjoyed.

HOW TO WORK
IN SOMEONE ELSE'S
COUNTRY

INTRODUCTION

As the process of globalization accelerates—for better or for worse—many professionals will find themselves working abroad. Opportunities abound for those who dare to seize them, for long-term postings as well as for short-term consultancies, particularly in countries where the needs are great and the available resources are few—the so-called developing world.

There are many reasons for seeking work in a foreign land, and more and more professionals are packing their bags, boarding the plane, and flying into the unknown. Likewise, more and more students are seeking overseas learning experiences. Most want to "make a difference" and look forward to the adventure of travel and to the opportunity for the rich experience of living and working in another culture. But many have unrealistic expectations and are unprepared for the situations they will face.

In order to be successful working in a foreign country, you need more than professional competence and good intentions. You need to know how to apply your skills in a completely different setting. It is easy to make mistakes when you begin work in an unfamiliar culture where you can't "read" the situation. It is also easy to trip up when you are expected to work in a situation where you only know half the story, at best. The opportunities to redeem yourself are few and far between, so it is essential that you get off to a good start.

The purpose of this book is to give you practical tips on how to be effective when you work in a resource-limited country, on how to avoid the common blunders that can cause grief all around. Drawing from the experiences of many international professionals, the book is written for all those who are ready to be part of the global community and enrich their lives, whether as international aid workers, consultants, missionaries, journalists, student interns, or volunteers.

It is my hope that the information in this book will help make your international working experience personally enriching and as professionally rewarding for you as it has been for me.

RELATIONSHIP IS EVERYTHING . . .
AND EVERYONE IS RELATED

Your first and most important job as an international worker is to build good working relationships. Quite simply, when you work in a foreign country, the quality of the relationships you establish will determine whether your assignment is a success or a failure. Nothing else in this book will matter if you don't get the relationships right. So this first chapter focuses on the basics of establishing and maintaining productive working relationships in an international environment.

Put first things first, and what comes first are relationships.
Assuming that you have the right technical skills for your assignment, everything else comes down to relationships. Even if you find you are not as skilled as you should be in certain areas, good relationships can help you get through.

Relationships are particularly important in non-Western countries where work tends to be more personalized. In these countries you may find that people are more interested in your personal qualities than they are in your academic and professional credentials. In some countries people don't want to do business with you until you have established a personal relationship with them, until they know you and can trust you.

So your first priority will be to get to know people and let them get to **5** know you. Show interest in the people you work with and make the effort to develop friendly relationships with everyone you come in contact with.

The key word here is *every-one*. In a foreign environment, the international worker will stick out like a sore thumb. Although you may not be aware of it, people will watch what you do and listen to what you say, often with keen interest. The "word" will quickly get around about you, and you want that word to be good. So be careful to treat everyone you meet with consideration and respect. If you are rude to the porter, you can be sure that he will tell the driver when he comes to pick you up, and if your driver is a friend of the minister of foreign affairs (as one of mine was—more on that later), you may land yourself in deep trouble.

VOICES FROM THE FIELD

In Macedonia, at the height of the Kosovo crisis, a priest from Catholic Relief Services came out and imme-diately set up Friday happy hours. It seems trivial, but these events drew the entire office, without fail, every Friday at 5:00 p.m., and became a tremendous source of stress relief during nonstop eighty-hour work-weeks. We got to know people from different departments who we didn't otherwise even have time to say hi to during the week.

Dave, Media Representative

Treat everyone as if they were related to the head of state—it could turn out to be true.

Treating everyone with respect is the right thing to do. It is also the wise thing to do, particularly in small, resource-poor countries, where every-one seems to know one another and where the people you will work with may be related.

There are several reasons why it can seem that "everyone is related," and the number one reason is that they often are. Those who are fortu-nate enough to have jobs, particularly in developing countries, will some-times use their connections to help their relatives find employment as well. It would not be at all unusual to learn that the cleaner in your office is the cousin of a major political leader. But, of course, no one will tell you this. One international worker told me that it took him two years to discover that the secretary he had hired was the daughter of the prime minister. So beware. Your words to the cleaner may one day echo in halls of parliament.

Don't gossip *with* local colleagues *about* other local colleagues. You could find yourself bad-mouthing somebody's favorite uncle.

I once worked with an official who was the butt of jokes due to his many humorous blunders. I laughed along with everyone else as local officials recounted his gaffes, only to find several years later that this official was a close relative of a respected colleague and friend. I can only hope that my friend wasn't present when we were joking at his relative's expense.

In countries where only a small segment of the population has had the benefit of a good education, you may find that many government officials and business leaders are members of a relatively small network of privileged extended families. Generally these families have been advantaged historically by reason of their sociocultural status, personal wealth, or political power. They, like elites everywhere, often have close personal, financial, and political ties and travel in the same social circles. So it should not come as a surprise if you learn that your colleague in the Department of Agriculture is the son of the chief of police and the husband of the daughter of the minister of finance.

You are treading on dangerous territory if you complain about one official to another.

Don't get involved in local politics.

Your local colleagues may confide in you and seek your support in local disputes. While it may seem like a compliment to be made privy to the "back story," it is unwise to invite such confidences. As an outsider, you may not know the "real" story and can put your work at risk if you align yourself too closely with one stakeholder or group of stakeholders at the expense of the others. These alliances may shift and can backfire on you. Build good professional working relationships with all of your colleagues and avoid getting embroiled in local politics.

Remember: How you make people *feel* is sometimes more important than what you *know*.

There are many competent professionals who fail at international consulting, simply because they make people feel bad. The way they behave makes people feel small and inadequate and somehow inferior. If you make people feel this way, they are not going to spend much time with you, if they can avoid it. I have seen people literally run from foreign workers, as described in the following excerpt from my journal.

JOURNAL NOTE

The new consultant, Sylvia, has been here with us for three weeks now, and I am very worried that this consultancy is not going to work out.

Sylvia is very confident and digs right into the job at hand. She is all business. She works fast, talks fast, and doesn't hesitate to ask probing questions. Poor James (her local counterpart) looks stressed out and nervous—when he is here, that is. But lately he hasn't been around much. The other day I saw him practically run out of the office. I'm sure that he is trying to avoid this new consultant.

For Sylvia, doing a good job means getting good data and producing good reports. Yes, we need the reports, but the purpose of the reports is to guide our action. I'm concerned that *there won't be any action* if our local colleagues don't want to work with her.

Today is Saturday, and both Sylvia and I were working in the office. James phoned me from another part of the building. He said he had a draft for me to review, but couldn't bring it to me because one of the doors was locked. I sent the driver to unlock the door and to let him in. The driver came back with the speech—alone. He told me that James didn't want to come into our office. Now I know for sure that he is making himself scarce because he doesn't want to work with Sylvia. This infuriates me. James is the one who has to do this work after she is gone. She thinks she is doing a good job. I don't know how I will convince her otherwise.

Pacific Islands, 1999

This story did not have a happy ending. I never did succeed in convincing Sylvia (not her real name, of course) that her relationship with James was a problem that was impacting on her effectiveness as a consultant. She just didn't get it. The fact that she made James feel bad didn't seem to be that important to her, and she never understood why I was making such a fuss. Needless to say, this assignment was her last one with me.

At a cocktail party I overheard a consultant talking about how poorly our organization had budgeted for her assignment. As I listened, I felt the blood rush to my head. Little did he know that, three years earlier, I had been involved in transferring funds from other country budgets just to support this project.

Theresa, International
Health Professional

Establish a good reputation on your very first assignment.

First impressions count. In international consulting, the reputation you establish on your first assignment may stick with you for years. The best way to get a good reputation from the start is to establish good working relationships with *everyone* you encounter.

International workers who maintain supportive relationships with their counterparts and clients are in great demand. Many times I have been approached by clients requesting that I recruit a particular person that they had worked with previously. Once a good relationship is established, people will want to continue to work with you. We humans tend to be more comfortable with the devil we know.

Don't let bad relationships fester.

If a relationship does seem to be turning sour, make the effort to repair the damage. Even if the individual has a minor role in the big scheme of things, try to mend fences. Bad relationships don't go away by themselves and can come back to haunt you. Don't let small hurts fester into deep wounds.

JOURNAL NOTE

I almost didn't come to this meeting—I'm so bogged down with the Country X proposal. But I am so glad to be here. I've already run into three key decision makers working in Country X, and I know them all. One is a professional I worked with in Country X over twenty years ago. She's now an official of the organization that I hope will fund my project. Another is a guy I worked with three years ago in my last country. It turns out that he is the one who will be reviewing the project proposals. The other one is a foreign colleague—a national of Country X, who I worked with years ago. He is now a high-level official.

Ethiopia, 2005

It's a small world. Don't burn your bridges.

Maintain good relationships with other professionals working overseas. I have been amazed at how fast a person's reputation travels from company to company and from country to country. Professionals who work overseas tend to circulate from one country to another and from one organization to another. Don't make enemies. The person you find annoying could turn out to be the person interviewing you for your next job.

Don't burn your bridges—ever.

THE FIRST STEP: FIGURING OUT WHAT YOUR JOB IS

Okay, you've got your first international assignment, now how do you start? What are the things you need to do before you pack your bags? The short answer is that you need to find out where you are going and what your job will be. This is not always quite as simple as it seems.

Find out where you are going.

The easy part is to learn about the country you will be working in. It doesn't take long to surf the Internet, do a bit of reading, and chat with those who have lived and worked in the country, particularly to chat with its citizens.

So a good way to start your assignment is to learn about the country's history, culture, geography, and politics. Do men shake hands with women? What is appropriate office attire? Do women wear slacks or skirts above the knees? Who are the current leaders and how did they come to power? Were they elected? Or is there a monarchy? Your knowledge about the country will help you to understand the contexts in which you will be working and will help you avoid making comments that are perceived as

VOICES FROM THE FIELD
I always learn "please" and "thank you" and a greeting in every language, if nothing else. I find it makes a real difference.

Dave, Media Representative **11**

ignorant or insensitive. This information will help you understand why things happen the way that they do.

The information you gather will help you even before your departure. For example, you will have a better idea of what you should pack and take with you if you have knowledge of the climate, the living conditions, the cultural norms, and the availability of consumer items in the country in which you will be working.

People will appreciate your efforts to learn about their country, and the knowledge you have gained will make your travel much more interesting.

Find out what your job is.

Now, this may seem straightforward. After all, you probably have a job description and/or a contract. But finding out exactly what your job will be may not be as easy as it seems. The job description (or "terms of reference," as it may be called) often gives only a partial picture of what will be expected on your assignment. That is why your first job is to figure out what your job is.

There are many reasons why you may need more information than what is written in your job description. These include:

▶   THE JOB DESCRIPTION MAY BE OUT OF DATE.

The recruitment process for international assignments is often lengthy. A lot can happen between the time when one of the stakeholders decides that a worker is needed and the time when the worker begins an assignment.

▶   THE JOB DESCRIPTION MAY BE VAGUE.

It may be that the person who wrote the job description (perhaps someone sitting in the head office) was not clear about what would actually be required on the job. It may be that *no one* is clear about the description.

VOICES FROM THE FIELD
I have seen some job descriptions that include so much that I am surprised they didn't add "world peace" to the objectives of the three-week assignment.
Patti, Development Professional

▶ THE JOB DESCRIPTION MAY BE TOO AMBITIOUS.

▶ THE JOB DESCRIPTION MAY BE BUREAUCRATIC AND GENERIC.

It may be that the job description is one that is used for similar assignments in different countries. This type of job description gives you a general idea of what the job is about but does not really tell you what you are expected to do.

On the other hand, you may find that your job description is so clear and specific that there is little leeway allowed and that a certain output will be required no matter what.

I was being recruited as a short-term consultant (four weeks) to identify gender issues on an HIV/AIDS project. When reviewing the project proposal, I realized that I could never accomplish the expected outcomes in such a short time and discussed my concerns with the project director. He agreed that the required outcomes were unrealistic and admitted that he and several others wrote the job description one evening over a nice dinner and several bottles of wine. As the evening wore on, they had included in the job description everything they could think of that would be good to know. Now the job description was approved and couldn't be changed.

Nancy, Gender Adviser

In either case, before you go, you would be well advised to discuss your job in detail with any of the stakeholders who can give you more specific guidance about the current situation and about what you are expected to accomplish. But don't be surprised if no one can tell you. You often have to figure out what your job is after you arrive.

Find out the "real" reason you were hired to do the job.

One way to find out what your job actually involves is to find out *the real reason or reasons* you were hired. Some are straightforward. Some are not. Some of the possible reasons are:

▶ THERE WAS A VACANT SLOT, AND YOU WERE HIRED TO FILL IT.

This is often the case with long-term assignments in international organizations. In these situations, the job may be "what you make it," or your organization may have clearly defined expectations about what you are required to do.

▶ YOU WERE HIRED TO SET
UP A NEW COMPANY OR
A BRANCH OFFICE.
This falls into the "straightforward" category.

▶ YOU WERE HIRED TO
GIVE EXPERT ADVICE.
These tend to be short-term assignments in which you are expected to provide specific recommendations. Longer-term assignments of this type usually involve working on a team with local experts. Whatever the length of your assignment and however much expert advice is wanted and needed, don't expect your recommendations to always be implemented. In most cases, it is your local colleagues and officials who will be the decision makers, not you.

▶ YOU WERE HIRED TO LEND CREDIBILITY TO A
(POSSIBLY UNPOPULAR) PROPOSAL.
Outside experts bring a certain degree of authority to a situation, particularly one that requires significant change. You may find you have been hired primarily to lend support for a controversial plan of action. If this is the reason you were hired or if people think this is the reason (even if it is untrue), be prepared for the resistance you will meet from colleagues who oppose the plan.

VOICES FROM THE FIELD
Before I undertook the assignment to develop a curriculum, I reviewed the files and learned that a long string of consultants had preceded me, all of whom had failed to produce a curriculum acceptable to the country. When I arrived in the country, I heard that officials were already making bets on how long it would take to sink yet another curriculum—mine! Knowing the history, I refused to make a single move without the full participation of the local educators. In the end, they didn't want to sink their curriculum—the one they had developed.

Joyce, Human Resources Specialist

▶ YOU WERE HIRED TO SET UP A CERTAIN SYSTEM OR TO IMPLEMENT A SPECIFIC ACTIVITY.

For example, you may have been hired to set up a certain computer system or to do an audit.

▶ YOU WERE HIRED BECAUSE YOUR JOB WAS INCLUDED IN AN INTERNATIONAL AID PACKAGE.

The donor country has hired you to oversee or administer the funds and/or the implementation of the project. The receiving country may not think that your job is required, and they may not want you there. But they may have no choice. Your job comes with the funds that the country receives.

▶ YOU WERE HIRED TO "BUILD CAPACITY" IN LOCAL STAFF.

"Capacity building" is an objective in many international assignments, particularly in long-term assignments. It may involve a formal teaching role or, more commonly, a mentoring relationship with local staff to strengthen their skills in a certain area.

▶ YOU WERE HIRED TO LEND A HELPING HAND.

In this scenario—a very common one—there are experts in the country who know what needs to be done, and who know how to do it. But there are simply not enough local experts available to do the work. Your job in this situation will be to help with the hands-on implementation and, in some cases, to be a role model as well.

Figuring out exactly *why* you were hired will help you understand *what* your job is—what you will be expected to do. For example, if you

---

VOICES FROM THE FIELD

In the early days of the AIDS epidemic, health workers were fearful of having contact with those infected with the virus. To break through the barrier of fear and the stigma required a professional who was not only an expert but a role model as well—a recognized professional who would demonstrate willingness to provide basic nursing care with confidence and safety in homes, clinics, and hospitals.

Sandra, International Health and AIDS Adviser

have been hired to lend a helping hand, your job is not to give advice and hold seminars and workshops; rather, your job is to roll up your shirt-sleeves and help *do* the work that needs to be done. This is a lesson that many international workers don't learn until it is too late.

You have probably been hired for more than one reason. Finding out all the reasons you were hired will help you know what is expected of you.

Find out who was there before you and what they had to say.

You may not be the first person hired to do this job. You may be one of a long string of foreigners who have been called in to tackle a particular situation or to implement a particular project. In this case, it will be wise to learn as much as you can of the history of the project. You will want to know what worked and what didn't. Any background information you can glean from reports about previous consultancies and from interviews will be invaluable in helping you figure out what you should (and should not) do at your new job. But don't be surprised if there are a lot of holes in the story.

JOURNAL NOTE

When our team was being recruited for this assignment, we were all impressed with how conscientious the consulting firm was. It was clear from the beginning that they were serious about hiring the right team for the job. They even flew our overseas clients to Washington to interview us. Never had this happened before.

Now we know why the consulting firm was so careful about whom they sent over here—the last team was kicked out of the country! It has taken us three months to find this out. Our local counterparts still haven't told us what the last team did that was so offensive.

I can't believe we weren't told about this before our departure.

Southern Africa, 1984

Don't believe everything you read.

The reports of previous international workers often provide useful background information. These days you can easily load volumes of electronic documents onto your laptop and take them with you on assignment. These reports are often well written and easy to read. But they may be wrong.

Beware of relying on the expertise of the expert you don't know. Don't learn too much before you go. You don't want to unwittingly begin your assignment with someone else's biases.

I went to a Caribbean country, and at the end of my first week I opened up the document considered to be the definitive work on my sector. It was well written and sounded good but was mostly wrong. I asked some local colleagues about it and they said, "Oh, yes, the consultant never left the hotel and flew to Miami on weekends." The report was fantasy.

My approach is to skim the reports first. Later, after my initial observations, I can tell which reports are worth reading.

Bill, International
Health Consultant

You don't want to lose your time unlearning the wrong information you have picked up in reports. Your time may be better spent listening to your local contacts.

Focus on what you *can* do, but don't over promise.

When you are discussing the specifics of your job activities, keep it positive. Focus on what you can do, rather than what you cannot or will not do. But don't over promise. *It is better to underpromise and overdeliver than vice versa.*

Expect ambiguities and relish the surprises.

Accept the fact that your assignment is a venture into unknown territory. No matter how much you try to learn about your assignment before you go, there will always be surprises. The information that you have been able to gather prior to departure will be useful, but don't forget—most of this is secondhand information at best. So keep an open mind and be prepared for surprises on the ground. After all, this is what makes international work so intriguing and exciting. Figuring out exactly what your job is will be an ongoing process that will continue long after your arrival in country. You may even find that your job changes over the course of your assignment. Successful international workers learn to live with ambiguity and relish surprises.

I went to Hanoi for the first time and was 95 percent sure my task was to help lay the framework for a graduate curriculum in public health, though there had also been some vague mention of the cost of medical education as a concern.

I arrived over the weekend and went to the Ministry of Health on Monday morning. When I met with the officials, they asked me if my slides were ready, because they wanted to translate them for the national workshop that I was leading *(surprise, surprise!) on the following Wednesday. It was an even bigger surprise to learn that the subject of the workshop had nothing to do with a public-health curriculum. Rather, the purpose of the workshop I would be leading was to determine the full costs of medical education.*

A couple of long nights, and all was well. But what I learned, after the fact, was that the consultancy was never about a public-health curriculum. It was only about the costs of medical education. The issue of a public-health curriculum never even surfaced.

Bill, International
Health Consultant

THE SECOND STEP: FIGURING OUT WHOM YOU ARE WORKING FOR

When you work at an international job, you may find that you have many bosses and many clients. Each of these may have different agendas and different expectations of what you are supposed to accomplish. So figuring out whom you work for goes hand in hand with the process of figuring out what your job is.

Know the organization you are working for.

When you accept a contract, you will be directly associated with the contracting organization or company. Just as the quality of your work will reflect on the organization, the image of the organization will reflect on you.

Before you accept an overseas position, do a background check on the organization or company that is recruiting you. Use the Internet to learn about its vision, mission, and objectives. Seek information and references from friends and colleagues.

It is critical to know as much as possible about the work, professional track record, and general industry image of the organization you will be working for.

Identify your clients.

There are some situations in which you may have more than one boss and more than one client. Consider the following example:

> The Botswana Ministry of Finance needs an expert in options. The U.S. government has contracted with ABC Consulting Firm to recruit and pay the salary of the options expert. You are the options expert who is selected and begin your work in the Botswana Ministry of Finance. Who is your boss? Who is your client? The private for-profit contracting agency that recruited you and sends you your paycheck? The in-country representative of the U.S. (or other) government, keeping in mind that the government is the source of funds for your salary? The person you report to at the Ministry of Finance in the Botswana government?

VOICES FROM THE FIELD

I applied for a job as a project manager with a consulting firm in the Pacific Ocean region. Following an arduous interview process and reference check, I was offered the job. Shortly thereafter, one of my colleagues who had given me a recommendation contacted me and told me that he had heard that this consulting firm had formal ties with intelligence work and urged me to carefully research the background of my new employer.

I searched the Internet and found a long list of other projects and programs the firm had managed. It was only when I researched the background of the members of the board of directors that I realized the close connection between the firm and intelligence interests.

On further consideration, I turned down the new position. Unfortunately, my personal effects had already been shipped, and I had to arrange for their return shipment at my own cost.

Bob, International
Development Professional

In this common scenario, you most certainly must meet the expectations of the person you report to in the Ministry of Finance. If you do not, they will have every right to complain about you to the representative of your home government. The job of the aid program of your home government is to have good relations with the foreign government. So complaints about your work from the ministry will be taken very seriously, and the contracting agency will be duly informed. The contracting agency is expected to recruit effective workers from the home government. If the home government is not satisfied with your work, the contracting agency's reputation will be in jeopardy, and you will probably not get recruited for another assignment.

In my work as an evaluator, I have found that one way to get clarity on the clients' expectations is to involve all the key stakeholders in the development of an evaluation plan from the beginning. If agreement can be reached about the evaluation process and about the intended outcomes, you can save much time, money, and confusion.

Virginia, Community
Health Consultant

So, the simple answer is that you work for all of them. In one sense or another, all of these stakeholders are your bosses and all are your clients. As an international worker, you will be required to meet the expectations of all of them. This may not be difficult to do if there is general agreement among all the parties involved and if you are able to facilitate effective communication with and between all these stakeholders.

Your job is to identify *all* of your bosses and all of your clients and to meet their expectations.

Decide who your most important client is and make that client's priorities your priorities.

The problem comes when there is disagreement among the bosses or clients about what you are expected to do. In this situation, the best you can do is to try to facilitate communication between your bosses and clients and negotiate a plan of work that balances their various demands on you. But sometimes it is impossible to please everyone, and all you can do is bite the bullet and decide who, among all the stakeholders, should determine your priorities.

When you work internationally, you have many different agendas to address. Your stakeholders may include one or more employers,

JOURNAL NOTE

The rector of the university approached me last week, asking that I lecture in some of the classes. One of the professors is ill and is not expected to return until next term. The rector is desperately short of staff.

The head of our project is not impressed. He says we are not here to do the university's teaching for them—we are here to start a new program. But the guy at the embassy, who is supervising this government-funded project, agrees with me. The rector has been very supportive of our work, and I think we should help him out. That's why we're here.

I've decided to offer to lecture in just one of the classes. This will help out the rector and show our goodwill, but will also leave me time to work on the new program. The head of the project still isn't impressed, but he isn't making much of a fuss either. So I think it will be okay.

Southern Africa, 1987

governments, agencies, or interest groups, both within and outside your own organization. These agendas may be different from one another, if not in outright opposition.

However you manage this, be sure to address the agendas of your foreign clients. Make their priorities your priorities. This is not as easy as it sounds. Sometimes the stakeholders include several different foreign clients, whose priorities and agendas are conflicting, and sometimes one or more of their interests are simply not within the intent of the assignment. In these situations you need to show interest and concern for the issues presented by all of these stakeholders while communicating in a positive way what you will be able to accomplish and whose interests you are there to promote.

Don't forget the client who is not at the table.

For those who are working in international development and relief, the persons whose interests you are there to promote may never be present at the table when decisions are made. Your job is to advocate for them or, even better, to find a way to bring them to the table.

I always keep in mind that who I am working for is the person who is never at the table: the poor rural farmer, the urban slum dweller, and the hotel porter who is carrying my bags.

Bill, International
Health Consultant

QUESTIONS TO ASK
BEFORE YOU START PACKING

Whether your assignment is for two weeks or for two years, you will be wise to gather as much information as you can about your destination and living conditions before you go. This will give you valuable information about what to take with you.

The information you have been gathering about the country and the culture will give you useful information about what you will need to pack. In addition, talk to your employer and to others who have lived and worked in the country. They will also be a good source of information.

Questions to ask about shipments and carry-on luggage:

WHAT IS YOUR SHIPPING ALLOWANCE?
Find out your shipping allowance at both the beginning and end of your assignment. Ask about penalties should you not stay the full length of your contract.

WHAT ARE THE CUSTOMS REGULATIONS?
Customs regulations vary greatly from country to country. Many countries allow personal effects to be imported duty free within the first six months of entry. Others do not.

Itemize the contents of your shipment. Keep original receipts of all goods, especially electronics. Take photos of valuables.

If possible, send an advance listing of your intended shipment to your new location, asking the staff there to read through the list and advise on any items or wordings that may not be admitted or that may raise red flags upon your arrival. Be certain that your inventory is in the official language of the country of destination.

When I shipped my goods to West Africa, my itemized list included the words "film" and "medicine/drugs." To my dismay, my goods were confiscated. The customs officials interpreted "film" to be movies, which must pass a censure board. "Drugs" required a special import license.

My baggage was not released from customs for six weeks—two weeks before my departure.

Bob, International Development Professional

HOW MUCH BAGGAGE WILL YOUR EMPLOYER ALLOW YOU TO CARRY?
HOW MUCH EXCESS BAGGAGE WILL YOUR EMPLOYER PAY FOR?
WILL YOUR EMPLOYER PAY FOR BAGGAGE INSURANCE?

For international assignments, employers will often give staff and foreign workers an allowance for a specified amount of excess luggage. Employers may also offer insurance on your baggage, above and beyond that offered by the airline carrier. Ask about this.

WILL YOU FLY BUSINESS CLASS OR ECONOMY?

Business class passengers are normally allowed an extra twenty kilograms of weight.

WHAT ARE THE AIRLINE REGULATIONS ABOUT BAGGAGE?

Airlines have different regulations about the baggage you can take on your flight and are becoming stricter in enforcing the regulations about the size and weight of both your check-in and carry-on luggage. Check with them ahead of time.

If you are transiting en route or changing airlines, carry sufficient hard currency (for example, U.S. dollars, British pounds, euros, etc.) to pay for excess baggage. Baggage rules are changing constantly in the face of antiterrorism security measures. Many airline companies will no longer allow you to check baggage to the final destination if there is an airline change or if you have more than eight hours transit time between flights or if you have an overnight stay. You may be required to pay excess baggage at each stopover.

VOICES FROM THE FIELD

My short-term assignment involved teaching in Indonesia, but most of the books and articles I wanted to use were not available in the country or were too expensive. So I asked for extra luggage allowance to bring the needed resources, and the request was always granted.

Jan, Nursing Professor

Questions to ask about your housing:

WHAT TYPE OF HOUSING WILL YOU HAVE?

Will you be staying in a furnished apartment or hotel, or will you be required to set up a household? Will your organization arrange housing for you? If not, will they allow you time during working hours to look for suitable accommodation?

The general principle is that you live at the level of your local colleagues. If you are a volunteer teacher working in a village, you would normally be expected to live in the same type of home as the local teachers. If you are working in a multinational organization, you would stay in a hotel or apartment of the same standard as your local colleagues enjoy. There is some leeway in this, but it is best not to deviate too much from this general practice.

WHAT CONSUMER ITEMS IN THE COUNTRY ARE
UNAVAILABLE OR EXCESSIVELY EXPENSIVE?

If you have a limited baggage or shipping allowance, be sure to pack the necessities that are not readily available overseas. Common examples of items that may not be available in some resource-limited countries include sports equipment for children, swimming suits, sanitary napkins and tampons, common over-the-counter drugs, well-fitting shoes, and computer and printer supplies.

It may not be worth it to pack your appliances if the electrical current in the country is different, which it probably is. On the other hand, if certain appliances are unavailable or prohibitively expensive and if you have a generous shipping allowance, you may wish to purchase transformers and pack these up along with your appliances. But first check to see that all of your converters or voltage regulators will handle the amperage of your appliances. If not, they will burn out. Remember that you need to check the difference in cycles (50/60) as well as the difference in voltages (220 is used in much of the world; 110 is used in the United States).

WHAT IS THE GENERAL STANDARD OF HOUSING AND SANITATION?

If you are traveling to a cold country, for example, where the hotels and houses don't have adequate heating, it would be wise to take a few hot water bottles to tide you over until you can purchase some type of heater.

JOURNAL NOTE

I packed all the wrong things. They told me that the house they had assigned to us was completely furnished and ready to occupy. Well, it does have basic furniture such as beds, tables and chairs, and the like. But there are no linens, no dishes, no cooking utensils. The last house we were assigned was fully equipped with all of these essentials. This time we were given a "settling in" allowance to buy what we needed. This would be okay, except for the fact that there are no department stores here. I will have to go from shop to shop, trying to find the items I need—and they are expensive. I have to deal with all of this time-consuming shopping at a time when I am getting the kids settled into school and starting a new job.

I should have asked for more specifics about the housing. The other members of our team seemed to know what to bring and have very few household items to buy. They're using their allowance to buy a good car.

Southern Africa, 1984

If the water is not safe to drink, you may want to take water purifying tablets or carry along a small kettle. You may also want to take a pump filter for camping or a faucet filter. You can purchase both over the Internet. They are expensive but provide protection against pollutants and toxins as well as nasty microbes. If you drink bottled water, buy carbonated or sparkling water. If it has "gas" you can be more confident that it is not just bottled tap water.

If you are in an area where there is malaria, it would be wise to take along mosquito nets and repellent as well as antimalarial medication. Look up your travel destination on the Web site of the U.S. Centers for Disease Control and Prevention (CDC). Then talk to your doctor or a travel clinic. Keep in mind that doctors in wealthy countries generally know little or nothing about tropical diseases, so they may find the CDC Web site helpful. If you get sick, be sure to let your doctors know where you have been traveling.

WHAT EQUIPMENT AND SERVICES DO THE HOTEL ROOMS HAVE?

If you can't start the day without your morning cup of coffee or tea and if there are no coffee-making facilities in your room, you may want to carry along your own heating coil or small kettle and a supply of coffee. Again, check the plug adapters, voltage, and amperage requirements of your appliances.

Examples of other things to check on include the availability of laundry facilities or services, irons, and hairdryers. If I know where I am going to be staying, I often phone or e-mail the hotel before my departure to ask what facilities and amenities are available, particularly on short assignments when I will be staying in an international hotel.

Questions to ask about phones:

WHAT MOBILE PHONES ARE AVAILABLE?

Does your new country have SIM cards you can buy? Will your

VOICES FROM THE FIELD
When working under field conditions in an area with malaria, I take a lightweight collapsible mosquito tent that is self-supporting with fiberglass rods and that zips shut and fits easily into a suitcase.

John, International Development Professional

current phone roam? If roaming is all that is available, the costs will be much higher, so include reimbursement for phone costs in your contract.

Questions to ask about your working conditions:

On some assignments, you will work in a comfortable well-equipped office in an urban area. On other assignments you may find yourself working out of your suitcase in a poor rural community without running water or electricity. Most assignments fall somewhere in between. Before you start packing, find out as much as you can about what your working conditions will be like and what resources will be available to you.

When I know I will be working in "the bush," I add Dramamine to my packing list, not only for those international flights but also for the unexpected in-country flights in a four- or six-seater aircraft, or for the twelve-hour ride in a truck on an unpaved road. I also take sun protection, including sunscreen, sunglasses, and a soft hat. I also carry a collapsible umbrella for protection from extreme heat and sudden tropical downpours and a small flashlight and battery-powered reading light in case of power outages (or no power). For minor health problems, such as low-grade upsets, I carry some over-the-counter antacids, and I always carry aspirin or an alternative for fever.

John, International
Development Professional

If you will be working under "field conditions," ask about the following:

WHAT COMPUTERS ARE AVAILABLE? WHAT SOFTWARE? WHAT PRINTERS? These days most international workers travel with their own laptops, but it is good to check on the compatibility of the various Windows or Mac-based software programs (unless you are running a newer vision of Mac with Boot Camp) so that you can make sure that you will be able to transfer documents easily. A flash memory stick to transfer documents is particularly helpful in the field. But if you expect to be transferring documents, install reliable, up-to-date antivirus software on your laptop to protect against viruses being transferred with the documents.

You also will want to know about the compatibility of the printers. Many people find it useful to travel with portable printers. Carry an additional power cord with multiple plug adapter fittings and a spare or extended battery pack for the laptop.

WHAT INTERNET CONNECTIONS ARE AVAILABLE?

Wireless connections are often not available. SIM-card-based wireless (3G/HSDPA) with roaming, if available, will be costly. An alternative would be to bring a telephone cord and a network cable. Also carry a device that you can use to connect your computer to the telephone outlet in the wall. Older telephones in some countries do not allow you to connect directly to the phone itself.

Things to pack no matter what:

CLOTHES HANGERS

Hotels rooms never seem to have enough hangers. Pack a few lightweight wire hangers that don't take up much room in your luggage.

ADAPTERS FOR ELECTRICAL OUTLETS

Electrical outlets come in many sizes and shapes—two prongs, three prongs, thin prongs, and thick prongs. Some prongs are straight, and some are slanted. Some are round, and some are rectangular. The variations seem to be endless. Find out what shapes are used in the country you are traveling to and buy adapters that will fit them.

If you will be traveling to different countries, buy a variety of adapters. These are available in the shops in large airports and are a very good investment. You can also buy an "international adapter pack" that includes most of the plugs you will need.

EXTENSION CORDS

If you will be working in a small hotel room in the field, an extension cord with multiple power points will be very useful. Many hotels have only one or two electrical outlets in the walls. So if you are trying to set up your computer and printer as well as turn on the lamp so you can see, you may have a problem. An extension cord adds weight to your luggage but can be a godsend, especially when you are working under field conditions. A lengthy phone cord for connecting to the Internet is useful as well.

A CHANGE OF CLOTHES IN YOUR HAND LUGGAGE

It is always a good idea to carry a change of underclothing and a clean shirt or blouse, just in case your luggage doesn't arrive with you—which on some flights seems to happen more often than not. The airlines are supposed to give you some shopping money when this happens, but they rarely do. Even if they do compensate you, it may not be possible to shop before your first appointment. It can be quite upsetting to start a new job or meet a new client wearing the clothes you have been traveling in for twelve hours.

VOICES FROM THE FIELD
When I arrived in Liberia, my luggage was nowhere to be found. The next incoming flight was four days away. I had no change of clothes and had to start work the next day. The local staff took me to the market so I could buy a dress and some underwear. We found a stall selling beautiful African cotton dresses. Perfect. One size. Very large. Cost: $0.75. A great bargain.

I wasn't so lucky with the underwear. I searched and searched and finally spotted a satin G-string in a "fashion store," neatly displayed under a glass counter. Cost: $5.00. The next day I started my new job in a tent of a dress and a too-tight satin G-string.

Taryn, Field Auditor

ESSENTIAL PRESCRIPTION MEDICINE

Bring along any medicine you require. You cannot count on finding the same medicine in the same formulation in other countries.

Write down the generic name of your medicine. If you do need to get a prescription filled in another country, the pharmacist may not be familiar with the particular brand name of the drug.

Customs officials may question you about any medicine you are carrying, especially if you are bringing a large supply. Keep a copy of your prescription and a note from your doctor among the documents you carry in your hand luggage.

BEWARE: Illegal "recreational" drugs should not be transported. In some countries the penalties are quite severe—even death. Do not take the risk.

A FEW PLASTIC BAGS

You will find endless uses for plastic bags while you are traveling. Ziplock plastic bags are even better. You can use plastic bags as trash bags and for packing; they are particularly helpful when you have wet clothes and dirty shoes. It is also useful to take a few plastic bags along when you go shopping in rural areas, since vendors may not give you anything to carry your purchases in.

Just think of all the things you do—even at home—with plastic bags. Imagine what you would do without any. In my early career, I worked in a developing country where it was almost impossible to get plastic bags. When we did get manage to get our hands on some, we hoarded them and carefully washed them out after every use so that we could make them last as long as possible. I have never recovered from this experience, and to this day, to the exasperation of my family, I still can't bear to discard a plastic bag.

A FEW SMALL SAFETY PINS

These are great for quick mending on the road and for closing the curtains of hotel rooms, which rarely seem to close completely and will let in a piercing light at dawn—not what you need after twenty hours of flying.

A SECURITY CABLE FOR YOUR LAPTOP

Although it is best to keep your laptop with you, sometimes you just can't, certainly not on a long-term assignment. A security cable that allows you to lock your laptop to a heavy piece of furniture or to a window grating is a must.

A SOFT, FOLD-UP, NYLON DUFFLE BAG

A duffle bag has many uses, especially on short assignments. You can use it for short field visits, when you don't want to take your large suitcase. You can use it to pack all the purchases you make when you travel. Most important, if your suitcase is torn, cut, or broken en route, you will be able to secure your belongings in the soft duffle bag and carry on.

A SMALL ALARM CLOCK

Hotel wake-up calls often come much earlier than requested, if they come at all. To be on the safe side, also set the alarm on your clock or on your mobile phone.

VOICES FROM THE FIELD

I have had hotel calls come as much as an hour before the time I had asked to be wakened. Better to rely on your travel clock or your mobile phone.

Dave, Media Representative

A SMALL FLASHLIGHT

Power failures in the developing world are common, even in the more expensive hotels. Being caught in unfamiliar surroundings in complete darkness can be unnerving. To be on the safe side, carry a small flashlight and a few spare batteries.

A SECOND PAIR OF GLASSES

Your glasses may be difficult to replace, especially if you are working in a rural area. So if you really need glasses, carry along a second pair. At the very least carry a copy of the prescription.

FOR WOMEN, A VERSATILE SCARF

A scarf is easy to carry along and is useful for many purposes. You can use if for warmth, for covering your head when necessary, and for dressing up a casual outfit.

ONE "GOOD" SET OF CLOTHES

Even if you are going to work in a refugee camp, you never know when you might need to dress up. Formality is important in many cultures, so you need to be prepared to dress formally when the occasion arises— often unexpectedly. Always take along one good outfit—particularly one that doesn't wrinkle. You may only need to wear your good clothes once

JOURNAL NOTE

What a surprise I had on this trip. It all started when I boarded the plane for this small, remote Pacific island, a flight I had taken many times before on previous assignments. The plane was usually packed with islanders and with tourists lugging their diving gear. But this day the flight was filled with people dressed in business suits, carrying briefcases and computers.

About an hour into the flight, I discovered why. Most of the passengers were diplomats and other officials on their way to the inauguration of the newly elected president of this tiny island nation, which was scheduled for the next day.

No one had told me about this, but if I had done my homework properly, I would have known. I knew I would be expected to represent my organization at the ceremony, and my first thought was, "What am I going to wear?" I had packed for work in sandy, tropical island villages, not for official functions.

Fortunately, I had brought along some clothes that didn't look too bad for the occasion—but they didn't look all that good, either. I've learned my lesson—always bring along something good enough to wear for that unexpected "special occasion."

Pacific Islands, 1990

a year, but when that one time comes, you will be so glad you brought them along.

It is easy to forget this. While I was writing this book, I participated in a meeting at a seaside resort in the country where I was working. The dress code was casual beachwear, so that was what I packed. But one morning when I checked my e-mail, I found an invitation to meet the First Lady and minister of education the next day. It took some scrambling to put together an appropriate outfit. I should have followed my own advice.

A FEW TRAVEL SURVIVAL TIPS

The following are a few odd tips to help make your life a little easier when you travel overseas.

Keep your passport up to date.

Many countries will not accept your passport if it is due to expire within six months. Some countries require that your passport has a certain number of blank pages. Check the entry requirements of all the countries you plan to visit or transit through and make sure that you carry a valid passport.

Secure your visas well ahead of time.

Check and recheck the visa requirements of the countries you are traveling *to*, as well as the countries you are traveling *through*. Some countries require that you have a visa if you are transiting there for more than a specified number of hours, even if you remain in the airport. Rules regarding visas can change very quickly, so don't rely on your memory or on your travel agent. Double-check yourself each time you travel.

Allow plenty of time to secure your visas. Sometimes you have to send your passport to the nearest embassy of the country you will be working in, and the nearest embassy may be in yet another country. This takes **35**

JOURNAL NOTE

Poor Kim. Her vacation in Fiji was ruined because her travel agent didn't give her the correct information. She was traveling to Fiji (with her baby, Michael) from South Africa and had to transit through Zimbabwe and Australia. She arrived in Zimbabwe as planned, but when she checked in for the flight to Australia, the airlines refused to allow her to board. The reason: she had no Australian visa. Her travel agent had not informed her that her layover in Sydney was one hour longer than was permitted without a valid Australian visa. Her trip ruined, all she could do was wait in the Zimbabwe airport until she could get a flight back to South Africa.

Southern Africa, 1992

time, and can be a problem if you need your passport for other travel. Citizens of some countries, including the United States, are permitted to apply for a second passport. This allows you to continue traveling on your original passport while the visa is being processed with a second passport. Contact the passport office or embassy for further information.

Carry your important documents in your hand luggage.

Don't place your documents in baggage to be checked, unless you can afford to lose them. This includes any reports or presentations you have prepared. The last thing you'll want to do is write them all over again. It is also best not to put cameras, electrical gadgets, or computers in your checked luggage, as these have a way of disappearing.

Scan or photocopy your passport and air ticket.

If you lose your passport or air ticket, it will be much easier to replace them if you can present a copy to the relevant officials. Scanned copies can be saved on your laptop and sent to both your home and overseas offices.

The wife of one of my colleagues recently lost her passport and found herself in the position of having to prove her identity. She was required

JOURNAL NOTE

I have been in Nepal for a week now, waiting for the airline to replace my stolen air ticket. Since my ticket was purchased from a travel agent in Botswana, getting it replaced is turning out to be a real mission. I had slipped the ticket under my arm while I was digging in my bag for my passport. Seconds later I realized it was gone. Good thing I have a friend to stay with here.

Nepal, 1988

to produce her birth certificate, driver's license, and marriage certificate. This took her weeks, since her home (and many of these original documents) was on the other side of the world. Save yourself the trouble and hang on to your passport.

Take along some extra passport photos.

You may need to apply for a visa or a permit of some sort during your travels, and a passport photo may be required. It is a good practice to carry a few extra passport photos along . . . just in case.

Keep a written record of the account numbers of your credit cards.

Be sure to jot down the expiration date and the three or four extra digits on the back of the card, as well as the credit card number itself. You should also write down the number to call in case you have to report your card missing. But if your card does get stolen and you don't have the contact number to phone, international hotels can usually give you the information you need. Credit cards get stolen all the time.

One trick is to disguise your credit card numbers by making them look like phone numbers. Give each credit card a code name and include it with your other contact phone numbers. You can also add the number to call in case you need to report that card missing.

Put your business card in your baggage identification tag and inside all suitcases and carry-on luggage.

If the baggage identification tag comes off and your baggage goes astray or if you leave your carry-on bags on board, the information on your business card will make it easier for airport officials to locate you. But in case your luggage should get into the wrong hands, don't include your home address or other personal contact details.

Mark your luggage for easy identification.

A brightly colored strap around your luggage will make it stand out from the others when it comes down the conveyor belt.

Secure your luggage with plastic wraps or locks.

In some airports you can pay to have your luggage plastic-wrapped. This provides some protection against theft—a big problem in some airports—and makes it more difficult for illegal substances, such as drugs, to be inserted into your baggage.

Carry bottled water with you whenever you travel.

You could find yourself waiting in small airports or bus depots where there are no safe drinks to buy. If you experience long delays or bad connections, you could get pretty thirsty and dehydrated. So always carry more

VOICES FROM THE FIELD

Our team was scheduled to audit two of our country offices, one after another—first India, then Pakistan. But halfway through the India audit we learned that our headquarters would not be able to arrange the Pakistani visa in time. So we decided to fly to Afghanistan and apply for our visas at the Pakistani consulate there.

The Pakistani consulate in Kabul was very efficient, and all went well until the official said, "Madam, please sign here and give me two passport photos." I was about to panic because I hadn't seen any places where I could get passport photos taken. Then I remembered that months earlier our headquarters had arranged for us to carry eight passport photos with us, "just in case." I dug around in my bag and managed to find them among my documents. Good thing—otherwise I don't know what I would have done.

Taryn, Field Auditor

water than you think you will need. Of course, you can no longer take water on the plane with you, but you can always give any extra unopened water bottles away before you pass through security. And remember that carbonated water is more likely to be safe than plain water (which could simply be bottled tap water).

You might even need to have your own water with you in international airports. One time when I was in transit in a South Asia airport, I tried to buy bottled water using the few rupees I had left over from my trip. I was completely taken aback when the vendor refused to accept the national currency as payment, insisting instead that I pay in U.S. dollars. Since I didn't have any U.S. cash on me, I was out of luck.

Carry your own sterile injection supplies in countries where medical care is poor.

In some countries, the availability of safe injection materials cannot be assured, particularly in remote areas. Where resources are limited, needles and syringes may sometimes be reused without adequate sterilization. If you expect to be traveling to countries where medical facilities are limited and medical care inadequate, carry a small supply of packaged needles, syringes, and tubing for intravenous infections. But check ahead of time that you will be allowed to get these through customs.

Bring along some dry snacks, such as peanuts, raisins, or a few granola bars.

Whether stuck in an airport or on an airplane without food, a couple of meal equivalents go a long way. But if you are traveling across international borders, don't take too much with you. Some countries don't allow you to enter with food of any kind.

One more tip: Avoid chocolate bars—they can get very messy when the weather is the least bit warm.

Take along some light reading material.

On long trips, after you get too tired to do the work you brought along, a little light reading may help you endure flight delays and other irritations.

Take a warm, comfortable sweater or jersey in your carry-on luggage, no matter how warm it is outside.

Your flight may be delayed, and the weather may have changed by the time you actually depart. It can be quite cool on the plane, particularly on flights in the tropics, when the flight crew turns up the air conditioning.

Carry some "hard" currency.

Don't assume that you can always rely on traveler's checks, credit cards, or ATMs. In developing countries it may be difficult to cash traveler's checks except at banks and large hotels that charge high commission rates. ATMs are not always available, or, if available, some accept only cards from local banks. Likewise, credit cards are not always accepted, especially by small shops and restaurants in rural areas.

Always have some U.S. dollars or euros in both large and small denominations, just in case. Interestingly, some countries will not accept "old" currency, and in some countries you get a different exchange rate depending on the denominations of the bills. For example, in some African and Asian countries, currency changers give the stated rate only for U.S. hundred-dollar bills. As the denomination gets smaller, the rate goes down as well.

In addition, carry recently issued currency, with updated security features. Many money changers do not have access to the electronic machines that detect counterfeit bills and are only able to do a visual test. So they will not change old bills. For example, in Indonesia in 2004, many of the money changers we encountered would not accept U.S. hundred-dollar bills that were issued before 2002.

Always carry a supply of U.S. dollar bills in small denominations, particularly when you are traveling to a small country or to a country in the midst of conflict. The airports in these countries may not have foreign exchange facilities, and the small dollar bills will be useful in case you need to tip porters, pay taxis, or pay a local to place a call on his or her mobile phone.

You may also need to pay some type of entrance or exit fee or "airport tax" when entering and leaving a foreign country. Some countries require that you pay in foreign currency, most commonly in U.S. dollars. Ask about these requirements before you begin your trip.

Unpack your clothes immediately upon arrival at your destination and hang them up to let the wrinkles fall out.

Wrinkles fall out quickly in the tropics because of the humidity. But where the air is dry, you can try this trick: Fill the bathtub up with hot water and hang your clothes on the shower rail or towel rack. The steam will work wonders on those wrinkles and will help warm up a cold hotel room as well.

KEEPING SAFE

You are more vulnerable when you travel to an unfamiliar country, so it is important to stay alert and take extra precautions. Thieves are on the lookout for unwary (and tired, jet-lagged) travelers and can snatch your bag or pick your pocket before you know what's happening. This happened to two of my colleagues, right before my eyes.

The first incident occurred in full daylight as we were crossing a busy street in Hanoi. My colleague had been shopping and had her cash in a bag over her shoulder. As we crossed the street a young guy on a motorcycle drove up next to us, grabbed the bag right off her shoulder, and whizzed off on his bike. That was the last we saw of her bag or her money.

The second time this occurred was in the evening on a street corner in Barcelona. One colleague set her bag on the pavement next to her, while we stood chatting, saying our farewells. Two young men suddenly

I had a close call on my way here. I was sitting on the plane, exhausted as usual on this long flight, and suddenly I had the vague feeling that something was wrong. I sat there for a while and then realized that I couldn't feel my money belt. After sitting there a few minutes, frozen in panic, I started looking around my seat for it. During my search I happened to turn around and look back toward the washroom. There it was, right in the middle of the aisle, with all my traveler's checks, credit cards, and cash. With a pounding heart, I sprang from my seat and retrieved it. It must have come unfastened somehow when I was walking back from the washroom.

In Flight to the Cook Islands, 1991

appeared out of nowhere, running past us. Before we knew what was happening, they grabbed her bag off the sidewalk and disappeared down a side street. That was the end of that bag as well.

You just can't be too careful, whatever country you're in.

Carry your credit cards, money, and passport in a money belt.

Buy a money belt in the airport or in a luggage shop and tuck it under your clothes. This is a little inconvenient but offers some protection in case the strap is broken or becomes undone.

Be prepared. Things happen—all the time.

Plan in advance the steps you will take when you arrive for your first visit to a "challenging" country.

Over twenty countries in the world are experiencing conflict (if not outright war) or are moving into post-conflict reconstruction. There is a lot of work to be done in these countries, creating a lot of international jobs. But consulting firms, companies, and aid agencies frequently do not have established offices, and workers coming into these countries often have to fend for themselves. This can be a real shock to the system for professionals who have previously worked only in stable environments.

Don't assume that you will be met at the airport. Things happen—or don't happen. You need a Plan B. Always have the telephone numbers and address of the key person to contact and the address of your destination in case you have to make your way there on your own. Have this information readily available when you go through immigration procedures. Often immigration officials will ask for the contact details of the person(s) with whom you will be staying or for the name and address of your hotel. Prepare a "constant companion" card for your wallet with all the essential contact information.

VOICES FROM THE FIELD

When I went to East Timor, I arrived late in the evening on a UN flight in a Hercules aircraft. There was no system for transporting our baggage from the airstrip and to the burnt-out terminal, and no attendant to help us. Fortunately, a kind UN volunteer who had been sitting next to me on the flight came to the rescue and helped me with my luggage.

Then I stood there in the dark, in front of the blacked-out airport, waiting for my ride. The darker it got, the more worried I got. I had no phone, and there were no phones in the airport. Finally someone from the World Food Program gave me a lift to their office, and I managed to call my office from there. It turns out that my organization had been told the wrong time for the arrival of the UN flight.

Joyce, Human Resources Specialist

Plan in advance the steps you will take from the moment you land until you arrive at your final in-country destination. This advance planning is especially necessary on your first visit to a town that runs more on informal than on formal ways of doing business. Find out how to get ground transport, where and how to change money, and how much to exchange. If you have an in-country flight, plan how you are going to get to the domestic airport, what time you need to get there, and what airline to use.

Try to look and act confident, no matter how confused you may be. If you act like you know what you are doing, you will be less likely to be targeted by those who want to take advantage of you.

Today when I got off the plane, there was no one to meet me. Since there were no chairs in this tiny airport, I plopped myself down on my suitcases, exhausted from the trip and jet-lagged from crossing time zones. I watched as, one by one, the other passengers were picked up by family and friends, but no one showed up for me. I knew the hotel that I was supposed to go to, but there were no taxis or buses. It was the weekend, so I couldn't call the office, and I didn't have the home phone number of my foreign counterpart. Even if I had, there were no public phones in the building. After an hour or so, when the arrival hall had emptied, one of the airport employees took pity on me and offered to drive me to town—an offer I accepted with much gratitude. So she and her friends squeezed me into her battered old car. I must get a gift for her to thank her for rescuing me. If it were not for her, I would still be there, perched on my luggage.

North Pacific Islands, 1994

Be wary of cab drivers, particularly in airports, who are not wearing uniforms or driving vehicles similar to those of the regular airport taxi companies.

Many taxis work independently and pay finder fees for "touts" who will approach you in the airport repeatedly and ask you if you need a ride. These fees are passed on to you in the end, often with extortionist interest to boot. If you are unsure, ask your employer or airport staff which taxis are best to use, to avoid problems.

Register with your embassy.

As soon as you arrive at your destination, be sure to register with your embassy. The embassy officials will warn you if the situation in the country becomes more dangerous for some reason and can help you out should you need to be evacuated. They can also replace your travel documents if they are lost or stolen.

Learn the location of the police stations.

Soon after your arrival, familiarize yourself with the location of the police stations in the areas where you live and work. If you ever suspect you are being followed, don't go to your residence. Go straight to the police station.

Lock up everything in your hotel room (at home or abroad) that you do not want to lose.

When you leave your room, lock essential items in your luggage. It is not necessarily the costly items that go missing, but the everyday items that you need and (depending on where you are traveling) may not be able to replace. Accept that some items will simply disappear. Valuables should go in a safe, if available.

On the day of your departure, store your packed baggage in the hotel luggage room.

Most theft occurs just before a guest checks out of a hotel. The thief assumes you will not notice the theft until you unpack at your next destination. If you do notice something missing, the thief figures that you will not alter your travel plan to pursue a claim, especially if you have a flight to catch.

On the day of your departure, don't leave your packed bags alone in your hotel room. To be safe, store your packed baggage in the hotel luggage room before you go to breakfast or leave for work.

Never leave your passport, money, or credit cards in your hotel room.

Unless there is a secure safe in your hotel room, check your money and travel documents into a hotel security box or keep them with you. In many countries, you are required to keep your passport on your person and are asked to produce it for almost any business transaction.

Report any theft to the police.

If you do have the misfortune of being robbed, go to the police station immediately. It will probably not help you get your stuff back, but you

Drive (and walk) cautiously.

When you drive (or are being driven), you are in more danger from the other vehicles on the road than you are from potential criminals. Road accidents, not crime, pose the highest risk for expatriates. Whether you are driving yourself, taking public transportation, or even walking down the street, you need to be alert to the possible risks. I say this from experience. I have been scraped by a bus in Mexico while walking on the sidewalk, and had a close call on a bus ride in the Andes when we collided with a truck coming around the bend. Fortunately these ancient vehicles moved very slowly, so I am here to tell the tale.

Travel risks are not limited to developing countries. One of my colleagues was killed while traveling on the highway in Europe. He was exhausted after completing a stressful assignment and traveling at a high speed. He may have fallen asleep at the wheel.

Be aware of the risks you are exposed to as you travel and take whatever precautions you can. Many risks are avoidable.

Get a phone.

The ideal is to bring a smart phone that roams in the country you are visiting. You can also bring a cell phone and purchase a local SIM card upon arrival. If you bring your own phone, ask your provider if the device you are using will work on the frequency of the country you are visiting and if roaming is available. Another option may be to rent a cell phone and purchase a SIM card at the airport.

Having a phone is good for security and will help ensure that you and your colleagues are in contact. Being readily available will help you get your job done.

Watch what you say.

Get a phone, but watch what you say on it. For that matter, watch what you say in e-mails as well, especially in countries with repressive environments.

Actually, it is wise to watch what you say anywhere. In one Asian country where I worked, all the foreigners were put on the same floor of the hotel, with a young clerk stationed at a desk by the elevator, recording our comings and goings. Needless to say, in this environment, we spoke with discretion.

Be careful whenever you discuss sensitive matters—someone just might be listening.

VOICES FROM THE FIELD

An embassy official once said to me, "Don't say anything on the phone that you would not want to see on the front page of the local daily newspaper."

John, International Development Professional

WHAT TO DO IF YOU GET THERE AND NOBODY WANTS YOU

Most every international worker will be able to tell you a war story or two about arriving at their destination, all excited and ready to "make a difference," only to be met by foreign colleagues who show a decided lack of enthusiasm, if not downright hostility.

There are a number of possible reasons why your counterparts might not be as enthusiastic about your assignment as you are. In fact, they might not want you there at all. If you can figure out why they don't want you, it will be easier to figure out what to do to turn the situation around.

You are hired to investigate or evaluate.

In some cases it should be no surprise that people on the ground may not be looking forward to your arrival. If you are there to do an audit or to conduct some type of investigation, you will likely be asking questions, requesting documents, conducting interviews, and generally interfering in the normal flow of their work by taking up their time. In some cases, you will be taking up space in crowded offices, as well. It should be no surprise that some of the people you are working with will consider you a nuisance, if not a threat.

True, you have to do the job you were hired to do. But there are some things you can do to ease the tension and create a more positive atmosphere for everyone. For a start, you can:

▶ Let people express their feelings. Don't try to defend the decision that sent you there.

▶ Acknowledge the disruption to the normal work schedule that the investigation, audit, or evaluation will cause.

▶ Try to be as unobtrusive as possible, and to minimize the disruption your presence is causing to the daily flow of work in the office.

▶ Investigate but don't interrogate. Ask questions patiently and with a nonjudgmental, matter-of-fact attitude. Allow people the time to fully explain their answers, even if you think some of the information is irrelevant.

The person who planned the job is no longer there.
It happens frequently in international development work that there may be a long lag between the time that the job was originally planned and the time that the funding is secured and the recruitment process is completed. The lag time could be several years. So by the time you arrive on

---

JOURNAL NOTE

Monday was the day my friends in the office downstairs dreaded—the day the auditor from Washington was supposed to show up. The local audit team had discovered irregularities, and now the big guns were being sent in. Those believed to be guilty had absconded to parts unknown, and these poor souls were left holding the bag.

Fortunately, the auditor, a guy named Brian, turned out to be a real gentleman. He parked himself in the small office assigned to him and started poring over the documents he had requested. The only time he came out of his office was when he had a question. They hardly knew he was there. He didn't even ask for a cup of tea.

But the best part about Brian was that he listened. When he uncovered an audit finding, he allowed the staff to explain.

Any time now our office will be due for an audit. I sure hope we get an auditor like Brian!

Southern Africa, 2003

Upon arrival, you could find that the official currently in the post may not think an international expert is required at all and may not know why you were recruited in the first place.

The local counterparts don't want to work with a foreigner.

In this situation, the senior officials have decided that an international worker is required and have proceeded with your recruitment. But your local counterparts, the people with whom you are expected to work on a day-to-day basis, don't want you there. There could be many reasons for this. For example, they might think that:

▸ You are not needed. They believe that they are perfectly capable of doing the job themselves, without an international expert—and they may be right.
▸ You will be an added burden—your expertise would be useful, but it is too much trouble to orient a new employee and to "take care of" a foreigner.
▸ You will show them up or expose their faults.
▸ You as a foreigner will never understand the situation.
▸ Your recruitment is an insult to them—it implies that the local experts are not sufficiently competent.
▸ You will be like past international workers, with whom they may have had bad experiences.

Your challenge in this situation will be to turn things around so that your counterparts see you as a supportive colleague and friend and a positive contributor to the work rather than a burden or a threat.

The local counterparts wanted another person hired—not you.

In the world of international consulting, friendships are formed and bonds are forged between international workers and the local counterparts with whom they work. This is one of the reasons international workers get repeat assignments in the same country—they develop good

JOURNAL NOTE

This was to be my dream job. I was hired by a prestigious international organization to be an adviser for an important national program in an exotic country. I was the envy of all my friends.

When I arrived, however, my local colleagues hardly had time to meet with me. Why, I wondered, if this program is so important, aren't people eager to get started working on it?

What I now have learned, after many months, is that my local colleagues were indeed interested in working on the program, but they were not interested in working with *me* or with any other foreigner. They felt they were perfectly capable of doing this on their own.

In the past they had suffered through a string of international consultants—some good, some not so good. The last one was good technically but tended to want to run the show. The director of the program did not want to have to deal with any more foreigners meddling in his program.

This being the case, the question was, if the director of the program didn't want an international consultant, why was I brought here in the first place?

I grilled my colleagues at the organization that had hired me, and this is what they finally told me. Three years earlier, a senior government official had requested that my organization budget for an international consultant, and he had had someone particular in mind for the job. But by the time the funds were budgeted for the position, that government official had been replaced. As a result, I ended up being recruited for a consultancy that the current officials thought was unnecessary.

Now I know why I wasn't greeted with open arms and why it has been such a struggle to become accepted as a valuable member of the team.

Western Pacific, 1989

relationships with their local counterparts, and the counterparts lobby
for them to return for subsequent assignments. This, of course, makes
sense. An international worker who is familiar with the country and
who has a good working relationship with the foreign counterparts can
quickly get on with the job at hand. An experienced international worker
with a good track record is highly valued indeed.

But it may be, for one reason or another, that you were hired for the
job, rather than a particular international worker that the local counterparts wanted and expected. Your challenge here will be to do such a good
job and relate so well with the people you work with that your counterparts will eventually be glad that you were the one selected for the job and
that next time they will ask for *you*.

Your local counterparts may not think you are qualified.

There are many reasons that you may not seem qualified to your
counterparts:

▸ Your educational degrees may be different from those generally held
  by foreign professionals in your field. This may be due to differ-
  ences in the educational systems of the two countries or it may be
  due to the fact that your degree and your work experience don't
  quite match up. Your curriculum vitae will be carefully scrutinized,
  so when you apply for an international job, carefully document all
  evidence that demonstrates that you are qualified for the specific
  international job you plan to undertake.

▸ You look (or are) young. In the Western industrialized world,
  youth tends to be valued—even glorified. But in many parts of
  the world, a few gray hairs will take you a long way. People are not
  very happy to have some fresh-looking kid giving them advice.
  Age often signifies wisdom, while youth may signal inexperience
  and even insubordination. This can be particularly problematic
  if a young person is in a position of authority in which he or she
  will be giving advice or instructions to an elder. So, if you are
  young, be aware that this could be a disadvantage. Take care that

your behavior and your appearance contribute to your image of a mature professional. Be unassuming. Ask questions of the older staff. Seek their advice. Do all that you can to make the older staff feel included and respected.

▶ You are the "wrong" gender or a member of an unpopular ethnic group. This is a tough one. The harsh reality is that prejudice and discrimination know no boundaries and come in many forms. If you find yourself in this situation, try not to let it undermine your confidence and get you down. In most cases, your counterparts will come to accept you as a person and respect you as a professional once they get to know you and see the quality of your work.

Your local colleagues do not support the project you were hired to do.

It is not uncommon that internationally funded projects are the result of agreements between a donor organization and a recipient organization—agreements made without the input or buy-in of those working on the ground who will eventually be expected to implement the project.

For example, a donor country may convince the political leaders of a recipient country to accept funds for a project that the officials on the ground of the host country have no interest in implementing. They may not want to implement the project because they think that it is a bad idea, because they think that it won't work, or because they think that it will cause them extra work. Whatever the reason, if you are the international worker hired to make sure that the unwanted project is implemented, don't expect to be greeted with cheers of welcome.

In this situation, your job will be to convince your local counterparts of the benefits (if any) of the project or to do what you can to make the project workable for the officials and beneficial for the recipients. This may involve negotiating with the donor to make the project more acceptable to the stakeholders. This is not a task for a rookie. If you find yourself in this situation, do not hesitate to seek advice from more experienced colleagues.

The devil is in the context.

Get the background information on your job. Your recruitment as an international worker may have been the result of a long consultative process, or it may have been the result of a last-minute decision; someone could have said, for example, "Before we extend this project, we need an evaluation." The more information you can gather about the context in which that decision was made, the better prepared you will be to cope with any resistance you may meet when you take up your assignment.

It will cost your organization a lot of money to send you on an overseas assignment. The organization will have to identify the resources for your international flight, for your salary, and for your living expenses. If you can find out who among all the stakeholders promoted this job and why, you will have a lot of valuable information about the context of your assignment—information that will help you convince your employers that they made the right decision in planning this job and that they made the right decision in hiring you for the job.

HOW TO MAKE THEM GLAD
THAT YOU ARE THERE

Whether or not your local colleagues wanted you there in the first place, your first job is to make them glad that you have arrived. The following are some dos and don'ts to help you get off to a good start in a foreign land.

DO start with who you are.

People will want to know who you are. In much of the world, this means who you are as a person. This differs from the West, where we start with our titles, university degrees, and job accomplishments. Talk about where you come from. Tell people a bit about your personal and family history, especially about your children. There will be plenty of time to let them know your professional experiences and academic credentials. Be a person first and the consultant part will take care of itself.

DON'T give the answer until you know the question.

Don't start giving advice the minute you arrive. Take time to get to know the situation. Although you may believe you are well prepared for this assignment and clear about what needs to be done, go slow. You may find that the situation on the ground is far different from what you had anticipated (and different from what you had been told).

A highly experienced consultant was hired to address a forum of new local development workers from West Africa. The consultant enthusiastically introduced his presentation with a series of colorful PowerPoint slides. About ten minutes into the presentation, a young African development worker raised his hand for a few minutes and then shouted out, "Please sir, please. Before you go any further—who are you?"

Taken aback, the consultant paused and apologized for not adequately introducing himself. He then stated that he was the vice-president of development, with thirty-five years of experience at an international relief and development agency. He added that he was also a lecturer at a leading U.S. university. Having finished his explanation, he continued with his presentation.

Before the consultant got another two or three words out of his mouth, the same young development worker blared out, "Excuse me sir. You haven't answered my question. Who are you?" Puzzled, the consultant was at a loss for words. Then another participant piped up and added, "He means, sir, we wish to know about you and your family. You failed to tell us who you are before starting."

The consultant caught the message. He turned off his PowerPoint presentation, pulled up a chair, and talked for twenty minutes about himself, his wife and children, and his passion for his work. The presentation then continued in an atmosphere of shared learning and open dialogue.

Bob, International Development Professional

Even if you have been correctly briefed and even if you know what needs to be done, you should still resist the urge to start giving advice. Your colleagues in the host country will not appreciate a person who starts spouting the solutions to their problems before he or she is properly briefed about the situation.

Listen, listen, and listen some more. Gently probe for clarification and then cautiously test your conclusions and advice. Preface remarks with questions such as "Does this make sense to you?" Or "My impression is . . . but I'm concerned that I may be missing something."

DO find out who's who and who does what.

Take the time to learn who the stakeholders are. The stakeholders are

JOURNAL NOTE

I can't believe this guy we recruited. I picked him up at the airport, and before he had even gotten his luggage into the car, he was lecturing me about the importance of "culture" and telling me about available resource materials, some of which I had read ten years earlier. I felt like a student in Anthropology 101.

I'm the one who recruited *him*. Not because we don't know what to do. We recruited him precisely because we *do* know what needs to be done. We would do it ourselves if we had the time and the staff.

Now I understand what my local colleagues put up with, over and over again, and why they are often reluctant to recruit consultants from overseas. Now I know how they feel.

Southern Africa, 1986

the decision makers, your colleagues, and those who are affected by the work you are doing and the recommendations you are making. For your assignment to be a success, many people need to be on board. Find out who these people are and learn their perspective on the work you have been assigned to do.

DO demonstrate your knowledge of (and interest in) local news and events.

When you first arrive, buy the local newspaper and tune in to the local news stations. Reading the front pages will inform you of subjects you can use to "break the ice" in conversations and will alert you to the "hot button" subjects to stay away from, such as political, ethical, and regional issues.

On the "stay away" side, information in the national headlines is good knowledge to have in one's head but not information to express to others until you are very sure of your facts and your audience. As a way of testing you, people may ask your opinions of these controversial political or regional issues. The wisest course of action is to avoid responding and to switch to another subject.

A good subject to switch to is sports. Read the sports pages and learn the names of the teams, the key players, and the major upcoming events. Many people feel passionate about sports and love to discuss their local heroes. Your knowledge of local sports shows your interest in the country and gives you a topic that can be discussed freely.

Reading the local newspaper and listening to the local news every day is a good way to orient yourself and get off to a good start in your new country.

DO find out what your counterparts expect from you.

In your discussions with your local colleagues, be alert for clues that indicate what they are expecting from you during this assignment. You may find that your colleagues' understanding of your assignment differs from yours. You may also find that the various stakeholders each have different expectations of you. Clarifying the expectations of the different stakeholders early in your assignment will prevent misunderstandings and disappointments later on. This is a dynamic process. Don't be surprised if the expectations change over time, as people get to know you.

DON'T rush it.

Often international workers arrive raring to go, with a long list of results and outputs to produce in a short period of time, only to find that their local colleagues don't feel their same sense of urgency and don't understand what the rush is.

Don't be dismayed by the slow pace of your local colleagues. Different people have a different pace, and different cultures have a different sense of time. So don't be discouraged and think no one cares about your work. That is not necessarily true. It may just be that things in that country move at a different speed.

It may also be that your local colleagues are so overextended that they find the additional work generated by your job more than they can manage. Find out about their other commitments and be reasonable in making demands on their time.

Don't let the pressures of meeting your target outputs create tensions in your relationships with your colleagues.

DO ask questions, but don't interrogate.

Some of your stakeholders will be very open and direct in sharing their concerns and perspectives and in telling you what they expect from you. Many will not. For this reason, you will need to watch and listen carefully for the nuances in what they say and do. This takes time and patience.

When you first meet your local colleagues, let them lead the conversation. Then follow up with some general open-ended questions. If you don't get immediate answers to your specific questions, leave your questions until next time. Don't let your initial interviews with your foreign colleagues seem like interrogation sessions. Don't make your colleagues feel like you are pinning them down.

DO beware of assessment tools.

Don't be a slave to the assessment tools that are so common in projects, with their predetermined set of questions and checklists. For many purposes (research being one possible exception), you can elicit the information you need in a friendly conversational manner, asking open-ended questions. Then if you detect reticence or resistance, you can transition to a different subject.

Confidentiality is never believed and seldom achieved. So asking for information in a written form or in a survey is often perceived as threatening. Unless your project requires it, use other methods for gathering information.

Certain questions are best asked in informal settings—over lunch or when traveling together in the car. Make the most of these opportunities.

DON'T record meetings.

Recording meetings can be very threatening to the people you are working with, particularly those in countries suffering from political unrest, conflict, or oppression. Recording an interview or meeting can also inject an element of distrust into the proceedings. While journalists and social science researchers commonly document information by recording it, this method is not usually appropriate for international project workers.

Today I visited the manager of one of our most successful rural projects. We couldn't have been more than ten minutes into our discussion when he started complaining about the "readiness assessment" that short-term overseas consultants had conducted the previous year at the beginning of the project. He complained that the assessment pamphlet had been at least an inch thick, and that the consultants had insisted on going through it tortuously, page by page, question by question, even though many of the questions were repetitive and clearly not relevant to this resource-limited rural setting. The whole process took two long days. He insisted that the consultants could have completed the assessment in half the time, "if they had used their common sense."

The fact that the local project manager is complaining about the initial assessment a full year into the project tells me that something is terribly wrong—wrong with the assessment tool and wrong with the attitude of the consultants.

Southern Africa, 2004

DO communicate an approachable, friendly attitude.

Your opportunities for informal contacts will be much greater if you are easy to approach and are friendly with your colleagues. If you give the impression of being constantly harried and too intense, no one will want to bother you. So try to lighten up, even if you are under pressure to reach your targets or to produce the deliverables.

DON'T be too high maintenance.

There are some international workers who have excellent skills but are simply not worth the trouble because they make too many demands on their organization and too many demands on their foreign colleagues.

Some workers expect the organization that hired them to "take care" of them; for example, by asking that the organization make arrangements for their holidays and attend to their personal affairs. Others require so much support, encouragement, or time that the organization will think twice before selecting them for another overseas assignment.

International workers can also be too high maintenance for their overseas colleagues. For example, some demand a better working environment than the local standard—a more spacious office, air conditioning, and so on. Other workers expect their local counterparts to take them on shopping trips and to tourist sites, and to help them with their personal errands.

It is one thing if your local colleagues want to socialize with you and offer to help you; it is another thing entirely if you are constantly demanding favors (or giving the impression that you are so helpless that you need them to look after you). This is taking advantage.

The bottom line is this: People who work overseas should be able to take care of themselves and should neither expect nor demand the creature comforts to which they are accustomed in their home country. Avoid becoming labeled as a high-maintenance worker if you want more international assignments.

DO find little ways to be helpful.

When people are working under difficult circumstances—particularly in resource-poor settings—sometimes what they need most is a little practical help. It is often the "little extras" that a worker does to help local staff that are considered the most valued contributions. The "terms of reference" or "statement of work" are often seen as "helping" the organization's objectives. But it is the personal assistance and help in meeting those objectives that earns the consultant respect among the local staff. The time spent on the little practical help you can provide will be repaid many times over in the cooperation and assistance you will receive in completing your "official" tasks.

Nice, just plain nice, will take you miles.

JOURNAL NOTE

Eric is the most popular consultant in our group. Everybody in the building likes him, and he is the first person they come to for advice and help. When their computers break down, he tries to fix them. When they have no transport, he gives them a ride home. When they are sick, he visits them. When they run out of photocopy paper, he gives them ours!

On weekends it is not unusual to see the local staff at Eric's hotel—the parents having a few beers, and the kids swimming in the hotel pool. He is an all-around good guy. It is no surprise that Eric has more influence around here than the rest of us combined!

Pacific Islands, 2001

LIVING AND WORKING IN THE PUBLIC EYE

One of the realities of international work is that you are always "on." Until you shut the door of your hotel room at night, assume that everything you say or do will be noted by those around you and passed on to others.

As a foreigner, you will stand out. People will spot you as a foreigner by the way you look or by the way you talk (your accent is a big giveaway) or simply because you are a new kid on the block. Everyone from the staff at your office to the hotel receptionist will be observing what you wear, where you go, and how you conduct yourself. An indiscretion or careless word could put your reputation and your work at risk.

DO be aware of the image you are projecting.
The choices you make in your lifestyle reflect certain values and will affect the image you project. The type of house you rent, the neighborhood you live in, the car you drive, the restaurants you frequent, the clothes you wear, and the people you associate with all speak volumes about you. Make sure that the image you are projecting is appropriate to the work you are doing. For example, it may be appropriate to stay in the best hotel in town if you are working with high-flying executives in a big corporation. But if you are working on a poverty alleviation project, you may want to rethink that choice.

JOURNAL NOTE

Jacob and I had quite a day. We each flew into the country for a one-day trip to discuss future projects with government officials. His flight arrived first, so the plan was that he would rent a car and then pick me up when my flight came in. As he tells it, he went to the car rental agency at the airport and requested, as usual, a small economy car. To his surprise, the rental agency gave him a free upgrade—a beautiful white car with a soft leather interior and all the extras. It was the most ostentatious vehicle I had ever ridden in. We joked about our good fortune and enjoyed every minute of our luxurious ride to the meeting.

The meeting was successful, and we decided to use our remaining few hours establishing relations with the people at the grass-roots level whom we hoped to engage in the project. As we neared our destination, it suddenly occurred to both of us that we couldn't drive up to their tumbledown office in such a fancy car. These people struggled to put food on the table. What would they think of us?

Feeling like criminals, we hid the car behind a clump of trees some distance away and walked over to the office, where we were given a warm welcome. But when it was time to go, we were confronted with another challenge—convincing these hospitable people not to walk us back to our car! Jacob and I won't make that mistake again.

Southern Africa, 2005

DO put on your "patience hat" in your interactions with the public.

This should go without saying. But all too often international travelers will lose their cool when faced with frustrating situations they don't know how to manage.

Be warned: Showing impatience will only reflect badly on you, no matter how justified you believe you are. If you lose your temper when someone pushes ahead of you in the line, it is *you* who "loses face" in most parts of the world, not the one who does the pushing.

Worse, someone who knows who you are could be standing there in the line watching your performance. So exercise patience. You don't want the word to get around that you're a rude foreigner.

DON'T discuss business in elevators.

I have been amazed to see otherwise sophisticated international workers walk out of a meeting and into an elevator and start talking to one another about what happened in the meeting—who said what; who was cooperative and who wasn't; how they did or didn't manage to get their proposal accepted; and what steps should be taken next. Meanwhile, people are getting in and out of the elevator, some of whom could very well be stakeholders (or associates of the stakeholders) in the very project being discussed.

Loose talk in an elevator is risky and could damage your relationships with local colleagues and your chances of success on the job.

DO be careful about what you say in the presence of drivers.

Similarly, careless talk in the presence of drivers is unwise. Drivers (like cleaners) are trained to be somewhat "invisible," and it is sometimes easy to forget that they are there. But drivers are very much there, and very much aware of what is going on. It would not be unusual for a driver to be a relative or friend of a government official or the head of your corporation, or, for that matter, a paid informant.

In some countries drivers are members of the secret service. In some communist and postcommunist countries, drivers have the same social

VOICES FROM THE FIELD

I was invited to be on a selection committee that was reviewing overseas applicants for a large health education project. One candidate was highly qualified and had worked in the country previously. It seemed to me that the objections to this person were trivial, but still he was not selected. After the meeting I asked a committee member, whom I knew well, why this doctor was rejected. I was told that when this doctor and his wife were in the country previously, they had short-changed their babysitter. It seems that they had arrived home much later than expected but did not pay the babysitter for the extra hours.

Eleanor, Government /
Church Liaison Officer

status as the officials they are transporting, and their salaries are not that much different either.

In resource-limited countries where jobs are scarce, your driver may be well educated, working as a driver simply because no other job was available. I have had drivers who were both well educated and well connected. One of my drivers had a university degree in political science. Another was a close friend of the minister of foreign affairs.

Don't underestimate drivers, and don't discuss anything within hearing range of your driver that you wouldn't discuss in public.

I was with some visiting Israelis in Ismailia, Egypt, the capital of the canal region where the Suez Canal Authority has its headquarters. One of the Israelis asked another if he had been there before. The leader of the Israeli group replied, "Yes, when I was driving a tank." Our driver allegedly knew no English, but I was not surprised to later learn that he was with the security services and that one of his purposes was to eavesdrop. As you can imagine, this was a very rocky visit.

Bill, International
Health Consultant

DO be cautious when discussing confidential matters in restaurants.

Discussing sensitive issues over drinks and a nice meal is a time-honored way to do business. But if you are discussing confidential or sensitive matters, try to arrange a table in a spot where you will not be easily overheard. Otherwise, as the evening goes by and the voices get louder, your conversation could become the main source of entertainment for the folks at the surrounding tables.

DO watch what you say in hotel lobbies.

A lobby in an international hotel is a beehive of activity, with drivers, porters, guests, and visitors going in and out, day and night. Hotel lobbies are very public places indeed. So unless you can find a secluded corner, this is not the place to discuss sensitive matters, either in person or on your cell phone. When you are standing in a hotel lobby, don't say anything you wouldn't want repeated.

JOURNAL NOTE

Today I went to the hotel to say good-bye to the consultant who had been doing some social research in one of the local communities. While we were waiting in the lobby for his airport transport to arrive, we chatted about his experiences in the country. He told me that this had been one of his most interesting assignments and then turned to me and said, "But I didn't realize the people here were so primitive."

I could have died. I quickly changed the subject and led him outside. As we walked out of the lobby, I looked around and noticed that a group of local women were within earshot. I can only hope that they didn't hear what he said.

It's hard to believe how a scientist could say such a thing—and say it in the middle of a hotel lobby.

Pacific Islands, 2000

DO watch what you say during your flight.

People often chat with fellow travelers during the dead time of air travel, when there is nothing much else to do, especially if the free booze has made them more talkative than usual. But beware. Loose talk to the wrong person can get you into trouble. On the other hand, "talking nice" can earn you a friend.

During my international flights I have found myself seated next to many travelers who could have either helped or hurt my work. These have included members of the press, government officials, relatives of government officials, staff from key international organizations, and CEOs from stakeholder companies. I've also found myself sitting next to colleagues from my own organization, whom I hadn't yet met.

I once sat next to the future minister of foreign affairs of the country I was working in. If I had made critical comments about the government or about his political party, I would have put my organization in a very bad position. Fortunately this story had a happy ending, and he became a very helpful supporter of our work.

Be discreet in your conversations with fellow travelers. Equally important, be careful about what the passengers seated around you may *overhear*. If you are seated with a friend or colleague, this is not the time to discuss confidential matters or to make joking or critical remarks about your organization or about the country you are working in. This may seem self-evident, but it happens all the time.

When you are flying to and from small developing countries, you need to be particularly careful what you say and how loudly you say it. In resource-limited countries, very few people can afford to fly anywhere. So the odds are that the people who do fly hold an important position or are related to someone who does. These people may not be next to you but may be sitting across the aisle or behind you.

Remember that you are always "on," even when you are traveling outside the country you are working in. Don't say anything to your fellow travelers that you wouldn't want repeated to a highly placed stakeholder.

JOURNAL NOTE

This evening I had a layover in Bangkok. While I was waiting at the airport for the hotel shuttle, two of the other waiting passengers struck up a conversation. One of the men was an agricultural consultant in South Asia. The consultant started talking about his frustrations with the department of agriculture and went on at great length about the department's inefficient bureaucracy, lack of forward planning, and so on, and about how his project would fix everything—if only he could get some cooperation. Finally the consultant wound down and asked his fellow traveler where he was traveling and what work he was doing. The consultant was shocked when he learned that the man was a senior official in that very department of agriculture, albeit in a different section. During the long ride through the Bangkok traffic, the consultant kept up a running monologue, trying to backtrack and make up for his earlier comments. The foreign official didn't have much to say. I wonder what happened in the end.

Bangkok, 1998

JOURNAL NOTE

It's been a rough week. Some international "experts" from the donor organizations came to conduct an orientation workshop for the field workers in our new project. These consultants were the ones that needed the orienting—not our field workers. Our local staff members are experts in their own right and know exactly what they should be doing. Nonetheless, all of us endured the presentations politely. Not so, the consultants. When it came time for the local people to present, the consultants didn't even pretend to pay attention. They started working on their laptops and hardly even bothered to look up. One guy even sat there sorting through digital photos of his kids. This behavior was worse than rude—it gave a message that what the local people had to say wasn't worth listening to.

Southern Africa, 2003

DO remember you are always "on" in meetings too.

If you have a job overseas, you can count on attending lots of meetings, workshops, and conferences—"talk shops," as they are called. Make the most of these events. Concentrate on the discussions and the interactions between the stakeholders. Watch how they engage in the decision-making processes. Even if you are knowledgeable about the information being presented and the plans being discussed, you probably don't know the nuances of the context affecting implementation. Avoid the temptation to open your laptop. Stay alert and engaged.

Remember that you are always "on." Watch your body language and the expressions on your face, especially if the media is covering the event. When the camera pans the audience, you don't want to be caught slouching in your chair with a scowl on your face.

DON'T overdo the alcohol.

In some cultures, getting a little tipsy won't be held against you. In others drinking alcohol is definitely out. But whatever the cultural norms, take care not to drink so much that your judgment becomes impaired. You don't want to put your work at risk by being indiscreet—by saying or doing things that you normally wouldn't—particularly at a business function. If you want to get smashed, do it with friends behind closed doors—not in public—and stay out of circulation until you are cold sober.

DO use discretion in romantic encounters.

Work and sex can be a dangerous mix, especially when alcohol is added to the picture. It is not a question of being a prude, but rather one of practicality and safety. Casual sex puts you at risk for HIV, AIDS, and other sexually transmitted infections. Use good judgment in your social relationships. Avoid the tangled webs that are created when sex and work are mixed. Don't give cause for scandal, even if it is unfounded. For example, in some countries, you may place your local colleagues in an awkward position if you are with them frequently, especially if you are with them in informal settings alone. Be sensitive to the cultural norms, and avoid behavior that could compromise your position in the country, damage the reputation of your colleagues, and even put your health at risk.

WORKING WITH YOUR
LOCAL COUNTERPARTS

In Chapter 1 we said that "relationships are everything," and there is no relationship more important to your work than your relationship with your local counterparts.

Your counterparts are the local employees that you are assigned to work with on a day-to-day basis. When your assignment is completed, you will leave the country. But your counterparts will remain and carry on your work. If you have transferred your skills to your local counterparts, your contribution to the country will continue, and you will have the satisfaction of knowing that you have contributed to the career development of your colleagues. Even when local counterparts leave the job after getting trained (a common complaint), most will remain in their home country and put their skills to good use there.

You have much to contribute to your local counterparts. Your counterparts also have much to contribute to you. Your counterparts are one of your greatest sources of information—about the job, about what happened before you got there, about who's who and what's what, and about all the whys and wherefores in between. Your local counterparts are also a valuable source of information about the culture—about what's appropriate and what's not, and about the most effective way to approach a given situation.

JOURNAL NOTE

My colleague, Paul, helped me out of a very difficult and embarrassing situation today. At the last minute I was asked to accompany an interagency team to Cambodia. I hadn't met the government officials we would be working with and had only skimmed through the background reports on the flight over.

When we first arrived, we were ushered into a meeting room and invited to take our seats at a long table. I sat down in the middle of the table. Little did I know that I was seated directly across from the most senior government official present. But it didn't take me long to figure it out, since he directed all his comments to me.

I hadn't realized that in meetings like this, the leaders of the two delegations sit in the middle of the table, across from one another. This official had assumed that I was the head of the delegation, since I was sitting directly across from him.

Fortunately, Paul, the actual leader of our delegation, is a well-experienced diplomat and was able to engage the official and divert his attention away from me. But I was very embarrassed. Next time I'll watch where I sit and make sure I get a proper briefing from my local counterparts.

Cambodia, 1999

If you develop a good relationship with your counterparts, they can facilitate your contact with other officials and can help you work your way through the system and help you understand why things happen the way they do. But if your relationship turns sour, your counterparts can block you and your work in a hundred little ways—and in ways not so little as well.

The purpose of this chapter is to help you build good relationships with your counterparts, even if they didn't want you there in the first place.

Make your counterparts your key advisers.

Your counterparts can help you in as many ways as you can help them.

So let them. Make your counterparts your advisers. Ask them for information. Seek their advice. Your counterparts may also serve as both your language interpreters and your cultural interpreters. Your counterparts can help you understand the background of issues and can advise you on a multitude of matters, including matters related to protocol—where to sit, what to wear, and whom to acknowledge. For example, if you are entertaining officials at a dinner, you need to know where to seat people. Should the special guest be seated next to the host, to the left, or to the right? Or across the table? The protocol differs from region to region. Ask your counterparts.

Be reasonable in your expectations.

You and your counterparts are in very different situations. You are in the country for a specified period of time, away from your friends and family and earning a reasonable salary. Your counterparts have relatives, social obligations, and personal business that they have to attend to. Some earn poor salaries and some even have to work a second or even third job just in order to make ends meet. Don't make too many demands of them.

In some countries I have worked in, even highly educated professional and senior officials earn salaries so low that they can't even afford to pay their children's school fees. For them a second job is essential. For example, in one country I worked in, I found it difficult to schedule a meeting with the medical staff. I learned that the government doctors worked only a few hours a day in the public hospital where they were officially employed and poorly paid, and spent the rest of the day in private practice.

When your counterparts are living and working under such difficult circumstances, you can't expect them to work as long and as hard as you do on your particular project. Even if your counterparts live in comfortable circumstances, remember that they have the demands of normal living. Be reasonable in what you expect from them.

Get to know your counterparts as people. Find out as much as you can about the context in which your counterparts live and work, keeping in mind that there is much that you will never know. But take it slow and easy. Don't pry. You want to let your counterparts know that you are interested in their lives, but you don't want to be nosy.

JOURNAL NOTE

We hired a consultant to organize a refresher training for professionals working in the rural areas. Local professionals were recruited to work as trainers. But when the consultant arrived, he decided that the local professionals were not competent to give the presentations, so he did all the teaching himself. But since there was *so much* to teach, he ended up keeping the local trainers and participants late every day, working himself to the bone. Three months later, when I spoke to the local officials about this hard-working consultant, what they remembered was that (1) he did not work well with the local trainers; and (2) that he kept everyone late!

South Pacific Islands, 1997

Share your life with your counterparts— but keep your troubles to yourself.

Just as it is important to get to know your counterparts as people, it is also important to let your counterparts get to know you as well. But use discretion. For example, if you are working in a resource-poor country with underpaid counterparts, don't talk about matters that show how much better off you are financially. Complaining about the high cost of your child's European tour when your counterparts are struggling just to pay their children's school fees is incredibly insensitive and serves only to reinforce the wide gap between their social circumstances and yours.

In most cases it is best to keep your troubles to yourself, especially when working in a poor country. Your troubles may be nothing compared to theirs.

Avoid involvement with your counterparts' personal job issues.

Your counterparts may tell you about their problems with other staff or supervisors and seek your support. Even worse, you may have two official counterparts who don't get along. In these situations, stick to business and avoid being drawn into their conflicts. The best way to do this is to

JOURNAL NOTE

Today the ministry rented a battered old bus and hauled us all to one of the outlying villages to showcase their successful environmental improvement project. Six of us were consultants from various development organizations and the rest were government officials.

I usually enjoy these jaunts. But today I was so embarrassed that I couldn't wait for the trip to end. Three of the consultants spent the entire two hours of the trip talking to each other about their expensive vacations to exotic locales, apparently unaware of how their conversations completely excluded the locals and probably made them feel even poorer than they are. The strange part of it was that two of them are good consultants and kind human beings who I assumed would have known better.

South Pacific Islands, 2001

avoid discussions about the behavior of other staff. Although it is tempting to listen to juicy gossip, you will probably be better off if you don't know the "inside story," especially when you are told only one version. Don't make the mistake of taking sides in a situation that you probably know very little about, no matter what people tell you.

Include your counterparts in planning and decision making.
Give your counterparts as much control as possible. They often know what needs to be done and have the skills to do it. In many cases, the only reason you were recruited was because your local counterparts didn't have the time or the staff or the funds needed for implementation. So involve them in planning and decision making at every level.

Decisions involving the project and the counterparts should be transparent. Never exclude your counterparts from high-level meetings where decisions are going to be made. After your departure, it will be your local counterparts who are most affected by these decisions and who will have to live with the consequences. It will also be your counterparts who will be responsible for the sustainability of the activities you have initiated. If they are not on board with the plans you have made, your project may start to fizzle the day you leave the country.

You can leave the job and the country when your contract ends or when the going gets rough. But your counterparts may have nowhere else to go and no other job opportunities. So if you find that they are more cautious than you would like, this may be why.

Never surprise or embarrass your counterparts.

Consult, communicate, and consult some more. Avoid a situation where a third party informs your counterparts of a recommendation you have made or an action you have taken. This could embarrass your counterparts and affect your relationship with them. Keep your counterparts continually informed and give them the opportunity to give you their views.

Communication can suffer when you are working under pressure and focusing on producing outputs. But if you neglect to work hand in hand with your counterparts, you run the risk that your project will fail. Communication and close coordination between international workers and their counterparts are essential to good relationships and effective outcomes.

Speak in terms of "we," not "I."

When discussing a project, think about what the team has accomplished, not what you have accomplished. Speak in terms of "we" and mean it. Always acknowledge your counterparts' contributions. Work together with them on reports and publications and include their names among the authors. You are there to facilitate the work of your counterparts— not to promote yourself.

Let your counterparts take the lead, but don't force it.

Encourage your counterparts to be the face and the voice of the project— the ones to chair meetings, to lead the group, to give presentations, and to represent the project to the authorities as well as to the community.

I have attended meetings where the international workers were so busy debating the issues and arguing with one another that the local officials—the ones responsible for the decisions and most affected by them—couldn't get a word in edgewise. Don't let this happen. It is the counterparts who should be debating the issues, with input and support from the international professionals. Encourage your counterparts to take the lead.

Encourage but don't insist. If, for example, your counterparts are reluctant to give a presentation because they are inexperienced or because English is their third or fourth language, offer to help them prepare their presentation or to give a joint presentation. Help them to take the lead, but don't put them in an uncomfortable position.

Be sensitive to other situations where your counterparts may want to "take a back seat"—for example, when sensitive or volatile issues are raised with the authorities. In these cases, you as a foreigner may have to be the hard-liner or the bearer of bad news. Your willingness to "take the heat" and embarrassment will not go unnoticed.

Be an advocate for your counterparts.

Many overseas assignments have a capacity-strengthening component, particularly those in developing countries. Due to workforce shortages, new graduates in these countries may be placed in senior positions. These young professionals may have adequate "book knowledge" but little hands-on experience. If you find that this is the case, work closely with your counterparts so that they can gain the practical skills that you have acquired over the years.

Look for opportunities for your counterparts to further develop their skills. Facilitate their participation in conferences, workshops, and other activities that will strengthen their knowledge base and help them make useful professional contacts.

Mentor your young counterparts so that they will be able to carry on with the work when you leave.

Be sensitive to the effect of your presence on your counterparts' social relationships.

There may be times when your presence, nationality, gender, or religion puts your counterparts in a potentially uncomfortable position vis-à-vis their colleagues, friends, or family. At these times, the counterparts may want to demonstrate "distance" from you in certain public situations. Be alert to these possible dynamics and be prepared to save your counterpart embarrassment by "disappearing" gracefully into the background. Don't feel offended. It probably has nothing to do with you.

Make your relationship with your counterparts a priority.

The international worker's most important professional relationships are their relationships with their counterparts. These key relationships need to be approached with sincerity, commitment, and diplomacy. Manage them poorly, and you risk your professional reputation as well as the outcome of your project. Manage them well, and your relationships with your counterparts can be some of your most rewarding professional experiences.

MEET THE PRESS

You may find that your work or project attracts the attention of the media. This might be because your project is controversial or because it has become the subject of public debate. In small countries your project may attract the media simply because the journalists are desperate for news. Whatever the reason, it is well to be prepared. Bad publicity is the last thing you need. The wrong story can put your work and your job at risk. On the other hand, the right message will promote your company or your cause.

When possible, it is usually best to have your counterparts speak with the press. But sometimes this is not possible. So here are some tips on how to get the right message out to the public.

Decide on your message.
This may seem obvious, but it is essential that all the people on your team know the key messages that are to be presented to the public. Decide on your messages and say them over and over again, no matter what questions you are asked.

Limit the messengers.
Assign one (preferably) or two people on your team or in your organization to respond to requests for interviews. The person who is the focal

point for the media should be a good communicator who has access to
information about the project; who understands the issues involved, particularly the sensitive issues; and who can speak with authority.

Make your message short and clear.

The media is looking for short "sound bites," short quotes (usually one
sentence long) that give the gist of the story in an interesting, dramatic
way. The average print quotation is one to three lines long. The average
radio quote is five to ten seconds long. Be succinct and memorable. You
could say, for example, "The reality is that this project is going to save
lives, and everything else is secondary to that." Or "People too often
speak first to what cannot be accomplished. This project is a monument
to what *can* be accomplished."

Give the media these sound bites using language that is understand-
able to the general public. Avoid acronyms and technical jargon that will
confuse your target audience.

Develop friendly—but cautious— relationships with the media.

If your work is high profile, you will likely encounter the same journalists over and over again. Get to know their names and contact details.
Give them a call when there is something to report, especially something
that would make a good story. This friendly contact with the media will
increase their interest in you and your story.

Relationships with the press need not be adversarial. Journalists are
seekers of information, and can be friends to your cause if you treat them
professionally and provide them with useful information to which you
have access.

Establish yourself as a reliable and credible source of information.

Once you have established friendly relationships with the media, help
them out. Be the person they are comfortable to call when they are looking for a specific piece of information, such as a statistic or a name.

A colleague of mine, who worked as a spokesperson for an international private voluntary organization, once called four reporters with a hot tip on an ambush in a conflict zone in South Asia. The stories ran on the front pages of all four leading daily newspapers, and he formed close ties with the journalists. As a result, over the next few weeks, they wrote several articles quoting his agency colleagues.

Avoid idle chitchat with reporters.

Watch what you say in your friendly chats with journalists. You may find your words quoted out of context the next day. Remember that when dealing with the media, nothing is ever really "off the record."

Provide short written statements.

Have a written statement to distribute to the media whenever you give a talk to an audience. Even if your talk is not a formal presentation, if the press is expected, have a short summary to distribute to them.

Scatter your main messages throughout your written statement. Journalists are on the lookout for "grabs"—short quotes that give a significant, interesting message in just a few lines.

When you are speaking in a language other than the mother tongue of the journalists, you run the risk of being misunderstood. If you provide a written statement, you will be far less likely to be misquoted, and will also ensure that the spellings of names and organizations will be correct in any resulting stories.

Prepare carefully for interviews.

Ask the reporter the focus of the story so you can anticipate the questions. Be prepared for the tough questions. If the story is to be printed, ask whom else the journalist has spoken with, as this will give you an idea of his or her intent and tone in writing the article. If it is a radio or TV interview, ask if it will be recorded, which allows you a bit more room for error. A live interview demands succinct and accurate information on the first take.

Arm yourself with facts. Have key statistics at your fingertips.

Don't overexplain.

Stick to the main points of your message. Don't confuse your listeners

JOURNAL NOTE

I am still in shock. What an experience! There I was, standing on the rooftop of the news bureau, with the city behind me and the camera in front of me, struggling to hear the distant anchor through the earpiece and reeling in disbelief at the questions I was being asked.

"Speak to the world," the cameraman said, presumably to give me courage. I guess it was obvious to him that this was my first live interview on cable TV.

I thought I had prepared well for this interview. The producer of the program had called me the day before, asking me about my work and expressing keen interest in my project. When I had asked him how the interview would be conducted, he had assured me that the anchor would be asking similar questions. I had all my statistics written on 3x5 cards and was confident that I was well prepared to answer the questions.

As it turned out, the anchor did not ask me one single question about the work I did or about the organization I was working with. Rather, he asked hot-button, hardball questions about the controversial social and political implications of the project. I knew that one wrong word, one careless phrase, would result in a serious setback for my work.

Somehow I muddled through and got my message across without offending either the government I was working for (my government) or the government I was working with. But it was tough going.

Now I know that when I go into these interviews, I have to be prepared for anything.

Southern Africa, 2003

with all the whys and wherefores, unless you are specifically asked for this information. Make your point in three to five sentences.

Here are some good examples. "What matters most is not that this forest is standing today, but rather that this forest is standing tomorrow. In the time it took me to say that, 800 trees in the Amazon were cut down." Another example is Abraham Lincoln's masterful Gettysburg address, "The world will little note nor long remember what we say here, but it can never forget what they did here." The entire Gettysburg Address, heralded by many as one of the most powerful speeches in United States history, was less than two and a half minutes long. Clearly Lincoln understood the power of being succinct.

Stick to what you know.

Avoid falling into the trap of speculating. Stick to what you know.

Don't be afraid to say "I don't know" if the question falls out of your expertise or catches you completely off guard. One excellent tactic, used constantly by politicians, is to turn the question into one you do know and answer it using your message—for example, "I can't tell you what it means ten years down the road for international trade, but what I *can* tell you is that it means 50,000 American kids will get a head start today through our new school feeding program."

Make your answers brief.

Keep your answers short so that the interviewer has a chance to get to the next question. A good interview is a lively question and answer session, not a monologue. During television interviews, keep your key messages or grabs limited to around ten words.

VOICES FROM THE FIELD
When I was working as a spokesman for a private voluntary organization (PVO), I was interviewed on live radio along with the U.S.-based ambassador of an African country that was being criticized for its slow response to an unfolding natural disaster. The interviewer calling from a studio in New York directed his questions at me, even though the ambassador himself was there on the line and was far more qualified to speak to the workings of his government and the problems that they faced.

My answer was, "I am not really qualified to speak to the problems that the government is experiencing. What I can tell you is that we have not experienced any delays on the ground, and we have reached 100,000 people with food and emergency rations thus far," which was the message I was trying to get across in the interview. The interviewer finally gave up trying to pin me down on an issue about which I was not qualified to speak.

Dave, Media Representative

Getting over silence is more difficult than you might imagine during an interview. Studies show that most people are uncomfortable with silences in conversation lasting more than three seconds, and have a tendency to fill this space with additional off-message quotes, often saying things they had not intended to reveal. Watch veteran journalists during their celebrity interviews and see how long they pause before asking a new question, hoping the person they are interviewing will feel pressured into filling in the silent spaces with juicy tidbits of information. Don't fall into this trap. Give your answer and wait patiently for the next question.

Give credit where credit is due.

Acknowledge all those who are contributing to the project or activity being discussed. If you are working in someone else's country, you are there because someone in the host country had the wisdom and foresight to identify the need for your skills or at least had the grace to accept that an expatriate with your skills should be recruited. Find a way to acknowledge local initiatives, plans, and persons who have influenced and facilitated your work.

Beware of potential pitfalls in working with the local press.

Professional journalists in some countries may not be as scrupulous about not reporting speculation or hearsay as you might expect. Such unscrupulous reporting—and sometimes even inventing news—happens in every country, but in some countries it seems to happen more often than not.

If you are concerned about being misquoted, it is acceptable to ask to see the quotations attributed to you that are going to be used in any article, though not perhaps to see the entire article itself. If the journalist refuses to let you see these quotes, it may be wise to ask not to be quoted at all for the story. Better to be safe than sorry if there is any doubt.

Where possible, focus on the positive.

Unless the purpose of your organization is to protest some particular policy or activity, it is generally best to stay positive and not criticize those who hold a different view. Don't focus on what others (organizations,

JOURNAL NOTE

Today I made the long trip out to the bush to visit Sister Mary Claire and the orphans she is caring for. Most of the parents have died with AIDS, and many of the children are themselves infected with HIV.

We always enjoy visiting Sister Mary Claire. Her warmth and can-do attitude in the face of so much suffering is an inspiration to all. But today we found her in tears. Local government support to the orphan center had been cut off—all because of a newspaper article. Sister Claire blamed herself.

This is how it happened. A local journalist approached Sister Claire and interviewed her about the work she was doing with the children. All the sister intended to do was to speak about the needs of the children and the work of the center. She didn't intend to criticize the government. In fact, she didn't say a word about the government.

But that's where she made her mistake. Sister Claire didn't say anything bad about the government, but she didn't say anything good, either. By neglecting to acknowledge government funding (little though it was), she gave the journalist an opportunity to focus the story more on what local government was *not* doing for these orphans than on what the sister *was* doing.

So the angle of the story was that Sister Mary Claire, an expatriate, had to do this wonderful work (there was a photo of her hugging an orphan) because the government couldn't or wouldn't do it. No wonder the local official who had facilitated funding for the orphan center was so incensed.

Southern Africa, 2002

company, government agencies, and so on) don't or won't do; rather, focus on what your company or organization *is* doing.

Tell the truth.

A convenient lie or distortion is almost certain to come back and bite you. Always be truthful.

Don't criticize the government.

When you are working in somebody else's country, it is always a mistake—a bad mistake—to criticize their government to the media or to try to show up their government.

Bad-mouthing your host government is a quick way to end your international career— if not worse.

Learn from the politicians.

Listen to radio and television political talk shows. Watch how the politicians interact with each other and with the interviewer. See if you can identify the following strategies:

▶ Watch how they say their message over and over again. No matter what they are asked, politicians manage to work their main message into their response. This is not an accident but a careful and deliberate plan.

▶ See how they manage to keep the interview friendly, even with an opponent.

▶ Listen to how they acknowledge their supporters.

▶ Note how skillful politicians are in avoiding media minefields.

The key to working with the media is to have a clear message and to say it over and over again.

Remember what you have learned from the politicians— you don't have to answer the questions you are asked. You can always shift the focus to your main message.

DRESS CODE FOR THE INTERNATIONAL PROFESSIONAL

The dress code in many countries is more formal than it is in Western industrialized countries. People sometimes think that they should dress more casually in a developing country than they would at home. New international workers in poor countries worry that if they dress up, they will show up the locals and make them feel bad. But actually the opposite may be the case. It is often "dressing down" that makes people feel insulted, because it is interpreted as showing a lack of respect.

Of course, what "dressing down" means depends on the circumstances in which you are working. Use common sense. Appropriate dress will depend on whether you are slogging through the mud in a rural area or attending a business meeting in town. There is no simple formula that will tell you what to wear, but the following guidelines may help you figure it out.

Respect the culture.

The clothes we wear are expressions of culture and reflect

VOICES FROM THE FIELD
After an unexpected change of plans, I found myself at the airport checking in to fly to Kabul. I wondered if I would need to cover my head with a scarf. I looked around at the people in line, and every single woman had her head covered, even if loosely. Question answered.

Taryn, Field Auditor

JOURNAL NOTE

Our young consultant has been here over a week now. She's very nice and seems to know her stuff, but the people here don't pay attention to a word she says. I think it's partly because of her age, and she certainly can't help that. But it would help if she didn't wear such short skirts. Women in this country wear dresses down to their ankles. I'm not sure how to approach her about this.

South Pacific Islands, 1991

cultural norms and values. You show respect for the culture by dressing in a way that is considered appropriate by the people you are working with. When you are preparing for an assignment, browse the travel guides and the Internet for information on appropriate dress. Once you arrive, look around and watch how people dress when they are going about their daily business.

VOICES FROM THE FIELD

When working in an Islamic country, I carry a scarf or shawl with me at all times, no matter where I am going or what I am doing, so that I can cover my head when necessary.

Joyce, Human Resources Specialist

You don't necessarily have to wear what the people wear, particularly if you are in a country where traditional dress is the norm. But if all the women you see are covered from head to toe, you should at least know not to wear short skirts and sleeveless tops.

Follow the rules.

In some countries there are actual rules (laws, in fact) about how people, particularly women, must dress. Be sure to obey them.

We all know that in some countries all women, including expatriates, must be covered from head to toe. For example, when traveling to conservative Islamic countries, women are advised to wear trousers and long-sleeved tops or jackets that fall at least to midthigh.

Many other countries have rules about dress as well. In Swaziland, for example, King Mswati III considers women wearing pants to be an "abomination" and disrespectful of Swazi culture. Women are banned from wearing trousers in the royal capital. A woman working in Swaziland would be very foolish to show up at a government meeting in slacks.

Find out the rules and follow them.

Ask your counterparts.

If you don't know what to wear on a particular occasion, ask your counterparts or other expatriates who have been in the country awhile. People may be uncomfortable with a question like "What should I wear to ____?" This is putting them a bit on the spot and making them responsible for your decision. A better question would be "What do people usually wear to ____?"

Dress modestly.

As a foreigner, you will be respected for dressing modestly. The general rule is not to show too much skin, and you will be wise to follow it. You want people to focus on the work you are doing, not on how you are dressed or undressed.

But be aware that the skin that you are not supposed to show varies culture by culture. In some island cultures, it is perfectly acceptable for women to show their breasts but taboo to have their thighs uncovered. That said, it would clearly be imprudent for the international professional to reveal her breasts. In such cultures, unless you are at a tourist resort, women should wear long shorts over their swimming suits before taking a dip in the sea.

When in doubt, it is better to be on the conservative side. Short skirts, bare arms, and revealing bodices are all inappropriate.

Dress up rather than down.

When in doubt, dress formally rather than casually. Wear clothes that can later be made to look more casual if necessary. You can always take off your tie or remove dressy accessories if the occasion requires it.

But first you need to find out what dress is considered to be formal and what is considered to be casual. For example, in some cultures pantsuits for women are acceptable for everyday wear but are not considered

formal wear. In these countries, women should wear dresses to formal
events, not pantsuits or slacks, no matter how elegant.

First-day fashions.

The dress code on the first day of meetings and conferences is generally formal. As the days go on, ties and jackets may be shed and the dress may become more casual. But opening sessions are important. Be sure your attire matches the occasion.

Formal does not equal expensive.

Casual wear is not necessarily cheap, and formal wear does not have to be expensive. So when you are working in a poor country—especially when you are working with an aid mission—clothing that is conspicuously expensive and elegant is not appropriate. You can dress formally, if the occasion calls for it, without flaunting designer labels.

Wear business attire to government meetings.

When you meet with senior government officials or business leaders, dress as you would in your own country—a suit and tie for men, and the equivalent for women. This applies even when you are on a field visit in rural areas. More on that later.

Going local.

In some countries, traditional clothes serve as comfortable alternatives to standard Western business dress. Examples include safari suits worn by men in some African countries, the *barang tagalong* embroidered dress shirts men wear in the Philippines, and the beautiful saris and *salwar kameez* worn by women in India and Pakistan. In most cases I wouldn't start my assignment wearing traditional clothes. But once you get a feel for the situation and a sense of how wearing traditional clothes would be received, this could be an option. As always, you need to use your common sense. If all your foreign colleagues are dressed in Western-style business suits, it would seem more than a little odd if you showed up to work in traditional garb.

JOURNAL NOTE

Today was the monthly department meeting, attended by line staff in headquarters and field staff from the provinces—mostly expatriates. The meeting itself was pretty uneventful—the usual stuff. But one thing struck me. As I looked around the long boardroom table, what I noticed was that the expatriates were all dressed in shorts and sandals, while the locals—even those working in the field—were dressed more formally, at least in long trousers and a collar shirt. Many were in ties. There is something wrong with this picture.

Pacific Islands, 2001

When you meet a VIP, dress like one.

Our work group was once invited to a function hosted by the president of a small developing country. One of the members of our team had worked late that day and had no time to go home and change. So she came straight from the office wearing her everyday work clothes. My counterpart took one look at this casually dressed worker and turned to me and said, "I bet she wouldn't dress like that if she was going to meet HER president."

There are times when your appearance is more important than your output. A good international worker needs to know when those times are.

Keep dress-up items handy.

In settings where the weather is sweltering and the everyday dress code casual, many experienced workers keep a spare jacket and tie hanging in their offices and other accessories tucked away in a desk drawer. That way, if they are called out to a meeting unexpectedly, they can quickly upgrade their attire.

The impression workers give is as important as the amount of work they do. The way you dress affects the impression you make. This is not about "power dressing." This is about dressing appropriately for the culture, the work, and the occasion.

I still smile when I remember our consultant coming across the lobby of the elegant hotel in high heels twice the size of her feet!

This is what happened. The minister had organized a special function at the most prestigious hotel to welcome the new consultant to the country, and she had showed up in sandals! Sandals are not permitted in the hotel, let alone at a ministry function, so she was stopped at the entrance by the guard, and an employee at reception went to get her a pair of shoes that the hotel kept for such emergencies.

The problem was that the shoes were far too big, and she could hardly scoot them along the marble floor. By this time, people were standing around the lobby, watching this show and holding their sides, chuckling. Luckily for her, the minister himself, coming in right behind her, rescued her and kindly ordered the guard to give her back her sandals, dress code or not. This was a generous gesture on the part of the minister.

Theresa, International Health Adviser

WORKING WITH GOVERNMENTS

Most international workers will work with the government of the host country at one level or another. Whether you will be working in collaboration with the government on a project or whether you simply need the approval of government regulators for your activities, you can expect to be interacting with government officials.

Many international workers, especially those from large Western industrialized countries, have had little or no experience working with high-level government officials, even in their own countries, and are unaware of the many protocols involved. They are often surprised to find the extent of government involvement in activities that in their home country would fall under the private sector.

The purpose of this chapter is to give you information that will help you develop a positive working relationship with government officials.

Respect government immigration requirements.

Most foreigners need a valid work permit (or official exemption) in order to undertake employment. Even missionaries and unpaid volunteers are usually required to have some type of temporary residence or work permit. Most countries require that you secure the necessary visas and permits prior to entry. Find out the immigration requirements and make sure you follow them. Don't get off to a bad start by antagonizing the immigration officials. Never forget that you are a guest of the host country and work there only at the government's pleasure.

Make courtesy calls.

Soon after your arrival in the host country, you should make courtesy calls to those high-level government officials whose portfolio will be impacted by your work. For example, if you are working on water and sanitation at the village level, you may make a courtesy call to the village chief or the district councilor. If you are an adviser on election reform, your courtesy call may be to a member of the cabinet or even to the office of the president of the country.

Courtesy calls are not detailed briefings. So this is not the time for you to discuss the details of your activities, unless specifically asked. Rather, courtesy calls are an opportunity to acknowledge the status of the officials you are visiting, introduce yourself and your work, seek advice, and win support. Courtesy calls ensure that key government officials are in the loop and are not embarrassed later when they hear about your activities from a third party.

During a courtesy call, you have the opportunity to communicate the overall goals of your assignment and to hear the views of important stakeholders. Courtesy calls also alert you to the challenges you may face in the course of your work. For example, if early on you find that key stakeholders are not supportive of your project, you will have time to do something about it, either by finding a way to win their support or by making changes in the project itself.

If you are successful in your courtesy calls, these government officials will have a good impression of you and your work and will spread the word to others. This may open doors to you.

Take your counterparts with you on official government visits.

Never visit government officials without your counterparts, unless your counterparts or the official arranges otherwise. This applies particularly to high-level contacts with government in which critical issues are being discussed and key decisions made. Never give your counterparts cause to believe that you are usurping their position or making decisions behind their backs.

Let your counterparts take the lead.

Your counterparts and other local colleagues should take the lead in meetings with government officials. Let the local people do most of the talking. Your role is to help your counterparts prepare for the meeting and to back them up. If you feel that your counterparts are not communicating clearly, find a way to add an example or additional information for clarification, without contradicting or otherwise embarrassing your counterparts.

Comment favorably on the support you receive from government staff.

In your contacts with senior government officials, look for opportunities to acknowledge the hospitality, logistical support, or any other type of cooperation or assistance you have received from government employees. This is one way you can express your appreciation to the government staff members who are working with you.

Avoid criticizing government staff.

All of us have come across government bureaucrats in our home country who seem to delight in blocking us at every turn. The bad news is that one or more of these tormentors can be found in every government office in every country across the globe. So be prepared to put up with the frustrations they cause, and resist the temptation to complain to their superiors. It generally doesn't help. Government officials don't want to hear expatriates criticizing their staff, no matter how justified the complaint, and may end up being more irritated with you than with the offender. So, unless the situation becomes extreme, it is best to take a few deep breaths and suffer silently.

Do exercise patience when dealing with the bureaucracy.

Even when government bureaucrats are helpful, the bureaucracy itself may seem designed to defeat you, either because it is dysfunctional or corrupt, or because you find the government systems just plain confusing. For example, in some countries where there are parallel systems of government, you will have two (sometimes conflicting) bureaucracies to deal with. These include countries with monarchies and those in which a strong political party wields the real power. In these situations, it may be difficult to get plans implemented, especially if the civil servants can be overruled by the members of the royal family or by the members of the ruling party.

Whatever the situation, no matter how frustrating, you must work with (and around) the realities as you find them. If this means going to a government office day after day, each time bringing another document you were not told about the time before, then that is what you must do. Persistence pays. Losing your temper doesn't.

Show respect for official channels of communication.

Do not go over the heads of government officials who are directly involved in the implementation of your project. You may get the rare opportunity to discuss your project with a high-level government official or political leader—an opportunity that could help move your project forward. If this opportunity presents itself at a cocktail party, involving a brief conversation about your work, fine. But if you yourself set up the meeting, it is an entirely different matter indeed. In this case, you must take your counterparts with you, as well as the key lower-level government officials who are directly involved with your project.

Even if you do manage to get high-level political support for your project, successful implementation will require the cooperation of the line officials directly responsible. In a very centralized government, political support can sometimes force the bureaucrats to cooperate. But, more often than not, political support is just words. You will need concrete support such as transport, supplies, and permits, and in most cases you will only secure these from the officials on the ground. Don't alienate the line officials by going over their heads.

JOURNAL NOTE

Yesterday we had a meeting of representatives of all the organizations who are working in the province on the AIDS pandemic. This
included international organizations, government officials, embassy
officials, and the like. During the meeting, the coordinator of the province's AIDS programs pleaded with us to coordinate our efforts with
her as well as with each other, and told the following story. For the
past year, she and the members of her department had been developing a proposal for a large AIDS prevention project with consultants
from a bilateral aid organization. The final draft of the proposal was
then sent to the donor for approval. For months they heard nothing
more, but she didn't worry much about it because she knew how long
approvals from overseas can take. Then last week she learned that
a delegation from the donor agency had met with the premier of the
province and that together they had agreed to certain changes in the
original proposal. She was furious and is still smarting from the fact
that neither the premier's office nor the donor agency invited her to
the meeting or even informed her about it. I pity the consultants who
are sent to implement those changes!

Southern Africa, 2005

Secure government approval before engaging in research.
Governments in the modern world do not take kindly to foreigners conducting research in their countries without permission. In most countries,
foreign researchers must collaborate with local academic institutions and
must submit their research protocols to the government for approval,
often through an official body established for this purpose. Many governments have now established boards to "govern" research, and the required
approval process can take months. Including one or two line items to
provide resources for government involvement in your research is one way
to ease the approval process and build solid, collaborative relationships.

There are many stories of foreigners conducting research with the help
of local experts and institutions, only to depart the country with their

I have been staying with Sister Barbara for a week now. She is a missionary nurse who is working with the local traditional healers. People here are too poor to buy most Western drugs, but they do have access to a range of plants believed to have medicinal qualities. Sister Barbara has learned a lot from working with the traditional healers and told me how very excited she was when some European researchers showed up in her area to analyze the chemical properties and study the effectiveness of commonly "prescribed" plants. The missionaries introduced the researchers to the traditional healers, helped them gather medicinal plants, and even allowed them to use their facilities. Then, after several months, the researchers left, promising to send a report of their findings. That was the last they were heard of. It has been over a year now, and Sister Barbara has given up hope. I feel bad for her. She is so disappointed.

South America, 1979

results in hand, never to be heard from again. This is blatant exploitation. International workers have an ethical obligation to conduct research in a way that strengthens the capacity of the local individuals and institutions and to ensure that the data collected is made available to those who can benefit from it. This should be specifically written into the research agreement and communicated to all involved in the research process.

Do seek permission for research through official channels. But don't expect an immediate response. The officials involved will probably want to consult with local as well as other expatriate experts before making their decision.

Obtain the required permissions before publishing your work or your research findings.

Most international organizations require that international workers and other contractors submit their papers for review and clearance prior to publishing their work. The document should have the clearance of both the funding organization and the relevant senior official in the host government. This ensures that all those who contributed are properly acknowledged and that nothing in the publication will damage the relationship between the organization and the government of the host country.

Local colleagues and officials who have contributed significantly to the work being described or to the preparation of the publication should be listed as coauthors or otherwise acknowledged in the paper. A word of thanks in your publication to the host government is always appreciated.

Avoid involvement with internal government affairs.

If anyone tries to involve you in internal government affairs, turn around and run in the other direction as fast as you can. Unless your role in the country is political in nature, stick to the job you were sent to do. Don't get mixed up in matters that don't directly concern you, especially sensitive affairs such as hiring decisions and conflicts between staff. Even though you may have strong views about, for example, disputes between certain government officials, and even if you think one of the officials is less favorable to your project than another, don't let yourself get sucked into the conflict. In the first place, it is not your country, and it is not your business. In the second place, more likely than not, you, as a foreigner, don't know the whole story and never will. Getting involved in internal government conflicts is a good way to ruin your project and could even get you kicked out of the country. It has happened before. Don't let it happen to you.

Don't argue with government leaders.

Above all, don't get into arguments with senior government officials. This should go without saying, but it happens, especially when international workers consider themselves experts in a particular technical area. But arguing with a government leader is unwise, especially in traditional cultures, in which a person derives status based on their position and (often) age, and it is considered disrespectful to openly contradict them. You may be right, but being right will not help you do your job if you have alienated the people in charge. You need to find another way to put your point across. Arguing with senior government officials is a good way to lose future assignments.

JOURNAL NOTE

Today I looked on in horror as the consultant I was supervising started arguing with the minister. I tried to intervene, but he didn't get the hint and kept arguing his point. This guy may be an expert in his field, but he sure doesn't know how to be a consultant. He still doesn't think he did anything wrong, even after I tried to explain it to him.

Pacific Islands, 2000

Don't gang up with other international organizations, agencies, or companies.

International organizations and agencies often need to collaborate and "speak with one voice" to avoid duplicating efforts or working at cross-purposes. But this cooperation needs to be managed carefully. You don't want to give government officials the impression that they are being pushed around by a bunch of foreigners pursuing their own interests. So cooperate with others who have the same goals, but don't gang up on the country officials. In the end, it probably won't work anyway.

Remember that you are representing your country.

Whether you like it or not, when you are living overseas, people consider you a representative of your country. In this sense, you are as much a diplomat as are the staff in your embassy, and your behavior will reflect on your country. Keep this in mind as you go about your daily life and work. On the other hand, unless you are representing your country in an official capacity, it is not necessary to defend or to apologize for your country's policies or actions. Stick to your job and leave the politics to others.

VISITING THE FIELD

One of the benefits of working overseas is the opportunity for interesting travel in distant lands. Field visits often take you far off the beaten path, where you can see firsthand how ordinary people in the country live and work, and give you the opportunity to gain an understanding of the realities on the ground. Most international workers are eager for this experience.

The purpose of this chapter is to give you some tips about how to make field visits a productive and enriching experience for you and your counterparts and for the people you will be visiting.

Be a gracious guest.
Don't let your trip be a burden to those working in the field. Plan well ahead. Try to schedule your visit at a time that is convenient for your hosts. When discussing your visit, acknowledge that you are taking time from people's schedules. Your hosts in the field may have taken a lot of time and trouble to organize your visit. Express appreciation for their efforts.

In small remote communities, your hosts may even organize a welcoming ceremony. At the very least your visit will probably begin with an introductory meeting and a cup of tea. Accept whatever food or beverage is served to you, even if you don't think it is safe. You don't have to eat or drink it.

Graciously participate in the activities your hosts have organized for you, even if they seem unnecessarily time-consuming. Hosting a foreign visitor is an important occasion for many people. Let them enjoy it.

Travel with your local counterparts.

Always make work-related visits with your local colleagues. It would be considered very presumptuous to go alone, particularly if the people you are going to meet don't know you. Your local colleagues will introduce you and explain your presence in a way (and in the language) that the people you are visiting can understand and accept. Your local colleagues will also help you understand what is going on around you and will help you out of any sticky situations you may encounter. Your local colleagues are a rich resource. Don't travel without them.

Find out what you need and take it.

Before you go on your field visit, find out as much as you can about the living conditions. Will you be in a hotel in a city or in a tent in the bush? Will you be

VOICES FROM THE FIELD

When traveling across town or into a rural area, I always take some water, some food that won't spill or be damaged by bumping along in the car, some toilet paper, an antidiarrhea drug like Loperamide, a bound notebook, extra pens, deet to repel insects, and my camera. I throw all of this into a canvas bag that I can carry or throw over my shoulder. This, and my computer, and I'm ready for anything. If I think we may get stuck or need to stay overnight, I add a change of underwear.

The other things I like are 1 percent hydrocortisone cream for that mysterious itch from a bug bite or who knows what in the middle of the night, and sleeping pills—not always, but if your hotel is next to the bar or an all-night bus station, or if the bed is miserable, I go with the slogan, "Better living through chemistry." A good night's sleep can make a big difference.

Bill, International
Health Consultant

traveling by car on a paved road or in a bus or jeep dodging potholes? This information will help you know what to take along with you. I always try to be as self-contained as possible. If I am going to be doing any writing or giving any presentations, I take everything from paper clips to butcher paper, from marker pens to staples. I have found it is best not to take anything for granted.

Similarly, for my personal needs, I try to make sure I have the essentials, just in case.

Ask permission before entering a rural village.

You may need the permission of the chief or community leaders before you are allowed to enter a rural village. Your counterparts will be able to advise you. The village chief will want to know who you are and why you are there. Don't skip this step. If you do receive permission, you are likely to be welcomed with food and dance. But if you enter without permission, there could be trouble ahead.

VOICES FROM THE FIELD
My students were assigned to conduct a community health research project in a rural community. On the first day they approached the village chief, but he left them sitting in the hot sun all day because they had forgotten to cover their heads with traditional scarves. Recognizing the error of their ways, they returned the next day with their doeks *respectfully in place. The chief happily granted them permission to conduct their research project in his village.*

Sandra, International
Health and AIDS Adviser

Find out the rules and protocols for using a camera.

Ask your counterparts about the laws and customs involved in taking photographs. As a general rule, do not take photos in airports, in government buildings, or around military installations, as the use of a camera in these areas can land you in jail. Ask permission before taking pictures of individuals, particularly rural villagers. Different cultures hold different beliefs and may have sensitivities in relation to photography. Many people are delighted to have you take their picture, particularly on a digital camera, where you can show them the image. Others fear and resent it, particularly if the photograph shows them in a humiliating or compromising position. When in doubt, ask your local counterparts.

Do not tour facilities or institutions without an introduction.

In most countries, your counterpart must introduce you to the person in charge of the facility or institution and request permission for you to be shown around. For instance, if you wish to visit a hospital, you first need to be introduced to either the matron (chief nurse) or the medical superintendent or chief executive officer, depending on how the hierarchy operates in that country. Your counterpart will explain the purpose of your visit to the person in charge, and this person will usually assign a staff member to walk you around. This is different from the typical Western hospital, where you can just wander around as long as you don't go into areas that are restricted, such as the hospital nursery or the intensive care ward. Your counterpart will understand the protocols and can facilitate your visit.

Tours are not the time for giving advice.

Do not start giving advice the first time you walk into an institution or facility. The purpose of your first visit is to gather information and get a feel for the situation. Commend your hosts on their accomplishments; ask questions for clarification; and make note of issues and concerns that you may want to address at a later date. If you are asked for advice or recommendations and think you know enough about the situation to be helpful, go ahead and give your advice, but only in general terms. Off-the-cuff recommendations are risky. It is better to consult with your counterparts and study the situation in depth before passing out too much advice.

Let people take care of you.

You face many unknowns when you go out on field visits, despite all your preparations, and it is easy to feel out of control. Your local counterparts may have planned the travel without consulting you about arrangements, such as where you will spend the night. They may even have made security arrangements that you didn't know you needed and don't quite understand.

JOURNAL NOTE

We have a high-powered consultant here, and I'm not sure how to keep him busy. Yesterday I took him to the referral hospital. He has just been appointed to a high position in international health and came here to orient himself to the realities of the developing world. The chief nurse gave us a tour, and the consultant made all the right noises, fussing over the babies and chatting with the staff. So far, so good. But then one of the nurses proudly showed him the new patient record system, and everything turned sour. After glancing at the records, he proceeded to tell her, point by point, what was wrong with the system and how it should be changed. The nurses responded with cold silence. It took only a few minutes for him to realize how he had blown it, but it seemed to me like hours. He is here for two more days, and I am having trouble arranging more meetings for him. I guess the word has gotten around about him, because everyone seems to be too busy to see him.

Pacific Islands, 1989

When your local colleagues are discussing these travel plans among themselves, often in another language, don't stress. They know that they need to take care of you. Relax and let them do it. If you are stressed out and constantly trying to figure out what is happening next, you will ruin the trip for everyone. Try to enjoy the fact that, for once, someone else is taking charge.

VOICES FROM THE FIELD

Traveling to our rural projects turned out to be quite an experience—the Egyptian tourist police accompanied us the entire time. One police officer squeezed into our vehicle with his gun pointing out the window. The other police followed us in an open truck. The language barrier made it quite awkward—we were practically sitting on top of each other in the car for hours but couldn't communicate. We never did figure out why this level of police protection had been necessary.

Taryn, Field Auditor

Take clothes you can dress up or down.

As mentioned earlier, always carry along a few items of clothing that you can wear to a formal event, because you never know when one may be scheduled. Even when you are touring in a rural community, be aware that this field visit is a special occasion for your local counterparts as well as for the local officials you may be visiting. For example, if you are scheduled to visit a local school, the principal and teachers will probably greet you wearing their finest. Your counterparts will probably be equally well dressed. Don't embarrass yourself or others by wearing a T-shirt when everyone else is sporting a jacket and tie.

Go ahead and be a VIP.

Your foreign hosts may consider your visit to be a great honor. This may be because foreigners rarely visit their community or because your local counterparts may have presented you as a very important dignitary. If you work for a relief organization, the people may see you personally as the source of desperately needed aid, and the gratitude they express may be overwhelming, as well as downright embarrassing.

VOICES FROM THE FIELD

The last part of our audit was to go to a small village in East Benin and observe the food being distributed to the intended beneficiaries. When the driver and I arrived, we waited in our vehicle until the village chief beckoned us. While we were waiting, he gathered the whole village into the main meeting area, an open hut with a thatched roof. Then we were invited to sit with him in the only chairs available. As we sat in front of the village, the chief expressed his appreciation for my visit to his village and thanked me for the food given to them. The chief then proceeded to tell me of the accomplishments of the villagers of which he was most proud. The children were curious of me, but shyly kept their distance. Then one little five-year-old, with a big smile on his face, bravely walked up to me and said, "Thank you for the food that fed my mother, father, brothers, and sisters." To the villagers I was the person providing the food. Just me. I was overwhelmed with humility. I was only the auditor.

Taryn, Field Auditor

Whatever the circumstances, let the people have the pleasure of hosting an important visitor, and graciously accept their expressions of appreciation. It won't hurt you to be treated like a VIP once in a while, and it may mean a lot to your hosts and your counterparts. Just don't let it go to your head.

PRESENTING YOUR MESSAGE

You can be sure that you will be called upon to make presentations and speeches while you are working overseas. Whether these are PowerPoint presentations in a corporate setting or talks to villagers from the back of a truck, you need to present your message clearly and appropriately.

Some people feel comfortable talking in front of groups. Others dread it. Most find that giving talks gets easier and easier as you gain more experience. The secret is to prepare well, forget yourself, and focus on relating to your audience.

When I give a presentation, especially when I've been called upon to speak unexpectedly, I am often reminded of a wise man's advice: Forget about yourself and make people happy.

So how do you give a presentation that will make people happy? Here are some tips.

Always be prepared to "say a few words."

As an international professional, expect to be called upon to give presentations with little or no advance warning. When you are on a field visit, when you attend a meeting, when you participate in a conference, keep in mind that someone may ask you to address the group on a moment's notice.

JOURNAL NOTE

I had the good fortune to travel with a government team tasked with conducting a technical assessment on one of the remote outer islands in the north Pacific. We sailed for hours on the open sea in a small aluminum boat. The journey was both scary and exhilarating. Upon our arrival, we were greeted by what seemed to be the entire village, who had gathered on the shore to welcome us with song and dance. I counted myself lucky indeed to have been included in this exciting venture—lucky, that is, until I realized that we visitors were expected to reciprocate and entertain our hosts as well.

The first of our party to step forward on the makeshift stage was a short man with a neurological disorder that had left his poor deformed body twisted in a way that was almost grotesque. He limped up, greeted the crowd with a mischievous grin, and proceeded to sing an old Elvis Presley song while strumming on his imaginary guitar and gyrating his hips in a most provocative way. It looked so ridiculous that I felt embarrassed for him. But the crowds howled with delight. Meanwhile, I was desperately trying to figure out what I would do to entertain the group when my turn came. Then, as the villagers were clapping and cheering, the short man turned to me and said, "It's all about making people happy."

I knew then that it didn't matter what I did as long as I gave the people a good time. So I did the only thing I could think to do and got up and sang the song I always sing when I am forced to perform—"Home on the Range." It didn't make the people shout and cheer, but it got me through the evening.

North Pacific Islands, 1996

This has happened to me so often that I am always mentally preparing myself to give a talk. When I am at workshops and conferences, I stay alert to the types of speeches that my local colleagues are giving, noting how long they speak, the issues they raise, and the general style and tone of their presentations. As I listen, I try to figure out what they would want to hear from me, a foreigner, if they suddenly called upon me to speak. Would they want to hear my advice, or would they just prefer that I say a few polite words of support? Once I figure out what is expected of me, if I am called upon to "say a few words," it is not too difficult to come up with something reasonably intelligent to say.

Prepare well and tailor your presentation to the target audience.

Show your respect for your audience by giving a presentation that makes it clear that you have given the subject some thought. This advice should be obvious, but far too often "experts" think they know so much that they can just get up and talk off the cuff. They may know their stuff, but their lack of preparation shows. You don't want to give the impression that the event or the audience wasn't worth the preparation time.

Find out as much as you can ahead of time about the people in the audience. Are they community leaders, business executives, or politicians? Will your audience be familiar with your topic, or will the subject of your talk be new? The more you can find out about your audience ahead of time, the easier it will be to prepare an appropriate presentation.

When I am scheduled to give a presentation, I try to arrive at the venue a little early so I can chat with the people as they arrive. This gives me a good sense of the different target groups in the audience, and, incidentally, also gives me time to scope out the setting and to make sure that my projection equipment works. I am more comfortable if I know ahead of time where I am going to stand to deliver my talk and where the projector will be.

Another advantage of arriving early is that it gives me time to scurry around to find out which VIPs are present and to write out a list of all the people I should acknowledge when I give my talk.

Avoid canned speeches.

Everyone can tell when you give the same presentation with the same slides that you gave in the last three countries you worked in. If you have a standard presentation, be sure to review it for its relevance and appropriateness for your audience. Add some country-specific information to

JOURNAL NOTE

I wanted to crawl under the table. This consultant, fortunately not from my headquarters, came to discuss a new child health initiative with the leading government pediatricians, some of whom taught at the medical school. Her canned presentation began with principles of public health so basic that you would have thought she was talking to a class of first-year medical students. It was worse than a waste of time; it was downright insulting. I was so embarrassed for her.

Pacific Islands, 2000

the presentation so that it doesn't appear generic. A canned presentation shows a lack of preparation and a lack of knowledge and interest in the local situation.

Be clear about the purpose of your presentation.
Is your objective to give information, to motivate, to inspire, to bring people together? A clear understanding of what you are trying to accomplish will inform the content of your presentation and will help you hit the right tone.

In many countries, meetings and conferences begin with formal "openings" and "closings," and it is important to get these right. If you are giving the opening address at a conference or meeting, the purpose is not to give a technical lecture. Rather, you should introduce the conference, telling the audience what they have to look forward to and explaining its scientific or social significance, and acknowledge all who have contributed.

If you are giving the closing address, discuss what the participants have gained from the conference and what this means in terms of future action. Above all, thank all who have participated, giving special mention to any dignitaries in attendance and any sponsors of the event.

Focus your presentation on the purpose of the event.
If this is a special day or a commemorative event, stick to the theme and give recognition to all who have contributed. For example, if you are

speaking on World Health Day and the theme that year is "Safe Blood," make blood safety the topic of your presentation, acknowledging and expressing appreciation for blood donors, the Red Cross, people who draw blood, and so on.

If you are speaking at the celebration of an achievement, express your admiration and respect for all that has been accomplished. If your organization has contributed to this achievement, be gracious. Focus not on what *you* have done, but on what has been achieved *together* with all the contributing stakeholders and how you will move forward *together*.

Put your presentation in context.

Make your presentation relevant to the wider context. You may wish to refer to the government's five-year development plan, the company's mission statement, or the organization's strategic objectives. This will show that you are knowledgeable about the background and the broader context and that you are working within existing frameworks.

Make your presentation relevant to the social and cultural situation as well.

Avoid being prescriptive.

Give information, present options, and let the people in the country decide how to move forward. Remember that there is much about the situation in a

VOICES FROM THE FIELD

During the first weeks of my very first job as an international health adviser in Africa, I attended a formal banquet with senior health academics and government officials. It was a pleasant evening and a good opportunity to meet many of the stakeholders I would be working with. As the evening was drawing to a close, I was shocked to hear myself being called upon to "do the closing." My mind went blank. I had never heard of a "closing" before, but I realized I had to do something. So I simply stood up and told the audience that we had come to the end of a lovely evening and that we could all now go home. Then the audience broke out into friendly laughter. I laughed too. Everyone knew that I was new in the country and obviously had no idea what a closing entailed, and I knew that I still had a lot to learn.

Sandra, International
Health and AIDS Adviser

JOURNAL NOTE

Today, driving today through this remote part of the country, I couldn't stop thinking about the presentation I had given on the International Day of Older Persons. It had been a walking event, so my talk was about how important exercise is to healthy aging. My presentation got wide coverage in the newspaper and was broadcast on TV and radio. Today, seeing old people climbing up steep mountains carrying heavy loads, I realize just how ridiculous it was for *me* to be talking to *them* about exercise. I'm half their age, and I wouldn't even be able to make it up the mountain, much less carry those huge loads.

South Pacific Islands, 1999

foreign country that you don't know and likely never will know, no matter how hard you try. Recognize that the people in the country are best placed to choose among the options and decide on the best course of action. Don't give the impression that you are selling one particular solution. Your job is to give people the information they need to make good decisions, not to prescribe a particular course of action, particularly if you are a development worker.

Be prepared to change midstream.
Despite your advance preparation, when you arrive at the venue and chat with the audience or listen to the other speakers, you may discover that the presentation you had planned does not suit. Perhaps your talk is too long or too technical. Perhaps the audience isn't what you expected. Perhaps the previous speakers covered all your points or the order of the speeches was changed because some of the invitees or speakers were late.

When you find that your presentation isn't right for whatever reason, change it. It is far better to speak extemporaneously than to give a talk that suits no one. You may have prepared a speech for community leaders, only to find that the organizers of the event have filled the audience with school children. Ditch the speech and talk to the children.

Acknowledge those present and express thanks and appreciation.

Begin your talk—whether scheduled or spontaneous—by acknowledging and expressing appreciation to all of the VIPs present, all of the people who have contributed to the event (including the other speakers), and all of the target groups in the audience. Such acknowledgments show that you understand and respect the authority structures of the society and that you appreciate the involvement of the community members. Acknowledgments are an essential formality, especially in most non-Western societies, and you will want to deliver them correctly.

Begin your acknowledgments with the most senior person present. It is best to acknowledge people by name. But if you don't know the individual names or can't pronounce them, refer to their status or position, like the Honorable Minister of Agriculture. The protocol for titles varies country by country, so check this out ahead of time.

There are different ways to make acknowledgments at the beginning of your talk. You may simply read off your list of people and groups to be acknowledged, nodding at them if you see them in the audience or on the podium. Alternatively, you may make some particular comment or express thanks when you give your acknowledgment; for example: "I would like to acknowledge with thanks the Honorable Deputy Minister of Home Affairs, who has contributed so much to the success of the work we are doing together." Another example: "I would like to thank all the people who have contributed to the workshop this week, especially the excellent trainers and the enthusiastic participants."

If you have been welcomed in a special way, if food has been prepared for the occasion, if people have sung and danced, a good way to start your talk is to mention them in your acknowledgments and express your appreciation. During the acknowledgments or at some other point early in your talk, you will also want to thank the organizers and the people who invited you to speak.

The acknowledgments you make at the beginning of your talk may be the most important part of your presentation. If you get this right, all else will be forgiven.

Refer to statements made by senior stakeholders in the body of your presentation.

Look for opportunities to quote or paraphrase statements made by previous senior speakers or refer to a policy position that a leader has held, such as "The Honorable Member of Parliament has made low-cost housing a priority. . . ." When there are a series of people speaking at a function, listen carefully and take a few notes so you can refer to what they have said and can respond to points they have made: "The Director of Transport has just explained the challenges of. . . ."

Where appropriate, look directly at the person you are quoting, and give a slight nod or hand gesture. This will show that you know who the senior stakeholders are and that you are listening to what they are saying. It will also show that you respect their opinions and are following their lead.

Acknowledge the media.

If members of the media are present, acknowledge them and make yourself accessible to them. Thank them for coming and, if appropriate, comment on their important role in educating and informing the public about your topic.

Make copies of your presentation to distribute to all the members of the media who are present. If your subject is highly technical, distribute a short summary written in lay terms. If you want the information you present to be reported accurately in the media, you will need to give it to the journalists in black and white.

Keep it clear and simple, but don't talk down.

Chances are that neither English nor French will be the first language of your audience and that they may have difficulty understanding your particular accent. So, whether you are talking to rural villagers or to scientific experts, keep it simple. Speak slowly, clearly, and distinctly. Use short, simple, declarative sentences. Avoid acronyms, jargon, or expressions that only native speakers would understand. Ask your counterparts to review your presentation to ensure that you don't use expressions or terms that would be unfamiliar to your audience.

Whatever you do, don't talk down to your audience. They are not children. Don't assume they know less than you do just because they speak another language.

Make it easy for the translators.

When speaking through interpreters, provide the translators with a copy of your presentation ahead of time so they can familiarize themselves with the topic and with the professional terms that you will be using. During your presentation, stop after every three or four sentences to allow the interpreter to translate your message.

When speaking spontaneously, without a written presentation, make a special effort to speak clearly and simply. Avoid negative and complex sentence structures, for example, "His intentions were anything but good." Your interpreters may not be professional translators, and you need to make it as easy for them as you can. Otherwise you may have a big surprise coming when you find out what they said that *you* said.

Limit the personal references.

A few personal references may be appropriate, depending on the topic of your presentation. But go light on this. The purpose of referring to your personal

VOICES FROM THE FIELD

I was the guest speaker at a grand ceremony on the steps of one of the country's great halls. The students were waving garlands as my translator and I were ushered up the steps. I stopped midway to greet the minister, who had come out to meet me. I shook his hand as we exchanged greetings and was then bustled off to the place where I would give my speech.

On the way home in the minivan, my counterparts couldn't stop laughing. This was unusual and puzzled me, and I asked them what was so funny. They said that when I greeted the minister, my translator's interpretation had been, "My, what a big hand you have." The minister, looking a bit surprised, had inspected his hand and said, "No, my hand is not so big."

I guess he wondered about what strange greetings these foreign women have.

Theresa, International
Health Professional

experiences should be to share real-world experiences and to add a human touch, not to talk at length about yourself.

Be especially careful to limit what you say about what you accomplished (or about what "they" did) in a third country. People find it irritating when international professionals constantly talk about what they did in this or that other country, as if whatever worked there would work in the present situation. Some discussion of your international experiences is useful and will probably be of interest to your foreign colleagues. But you will not win any points if you are continually telling people "how we did it" in another country.

Rather too short than too long

Find out how long you are expected to speak and keep to your allotted time. People want to hear enough from you to know that you consider them worthy of your time and your effort, but not so much that you bore them or that you eat into the time allocated to other speakers.

In most countries the most important person speaks last and longest, and in most circumstances this will be the local expert or dignitary. Don't cut into their time.

Not too informal.

When giving your presentation, don't be so formal and stiff that you seem distant and arrogant, but don't be too informal either. I can't tell you how often I have heard workers refer to the audience as "you guys." These good-hearted folk think that being informal makes them seem friendly and approachable, and they may be correct. But their informality may also make them seem undignified and lacking in respect for the occasion as well as for the audience. Listen to the tone and level of formality in the other speeches, and take your lead from them. Don't forget to watch your body language—it may speak louder than your words. Be as professional as you would be in your home country.

VOICES FROM THE FIELD
Some good advice that I never forgot: Start with a bang, end with a bang, and keep the bangs close together!

Sandra, International Health and AIDS Adviser

JOURNAL NOTE

Yesterday another expert from our head office arrived on the scene. His purpose was to give the keynote address at our workshop and to give us expert advice. There he stood—hands in his pockets, chest puffed out, speaking off the top of his head. Clearly he hadn't bothered to prepare. He rambled on about internal organizational matters of no interest or relevance to the participants. In fact, I am sure these field workers didn't have a clue what he was talking about.

Pacific Islands , 2001

What if they ask you for money?

If your organization or company provides financial support, it is possible that previous speakers will ask for more money or will specifically request that you fund something that they need, such as piped water for their village. If this happens—and it has happened to me on numerous occasions—you need to respond, even if you can't deliver the goods. Find a way to let your audience know that you heard their request and respond in a way that will be viewed positively without making a commitment that you can't meet. Even if you don't have the resources to meet their request, say a brief word about what you *can* do, even if it is only to help them find another source of funding. For example, "We admire the work X is doing and hope funds will continue to be available to expand this successful operation."

Keep it short, but say something. The worst thing you can do is pretend that you didn't hear their request.

Give listeners a message to "take home."

Whatever the specific content of my presentation, I always try to give the people in the audience at least one message that they can "take home." Amidst all the formalities and diplomacies, I want to give the audience some pearl of information or inspiration that will help them live a better life. Especially in countries where resources are limited and learning opportunities are few, I want to believe that the presentations I give are more than just "talk." The yardstick I use to measure that is to ask myself, "Was it a good use of scarce resources to bring people here to listen to me?"

Use the opportunity to give a message of hope.

Focus on the positive. You don't need to carry on about what is wrong—in most cases the local people know the problems better than you do—so leave the criticizing to them. Your job is to be encouraging.

In many parts of the world, even highly educated people work hard under difficult circumstances, for low pay and very little thanks. Your understanding of their situation and your recognition of their achievements will mean a lot to them.

Give a message of hope and inspiration. Tell stories of local "heroes" who have made a difference and who have received international recognition. Remind your audience of their successes. Make them proud.

Leave your audience with the feeling that they can accomplish even more.

Speak from the heart.

Talk *to* your audience—to all of your audiences—and speak from the heart. Remember the old saying, "People don't care what you know until they know that you care." Show that you care by the tone of your voice, by the effort you make to give a useful presentation, by the modest, dignified attitude you display, and by the respect you show for the people and their culture. People will forget your blunders—and you *will* make blunders—if you give a message of hope and speak from the heart.

Begin and end with the magic words—thank you.

You can't say "thank you" too often. Just as your mother taught you, these words are magic.

Just as you should begin your presentation with acknowledgments and thanks, you should also conclude your talk by thanking all those who contributed to the work you are presenting, and by thanking your audience for their attention. You will also want to thank any donor organizations that have provided funding for your work, either at the beginning of your presentation or at the end. You may find that someone in the audience thanks you as well. In many countries, it is the tradition to give a "vote of thanks"—words of appreciation to a guest speaker or to the organizer at the closing of a conference or meeting.

When in doubt, say "thank you." These words may be the most important part of your speech.

ON GIFT GIVING

Corruption is a scourge in many parts of the world. Corrupt practices are a key obstacle to development, contributing to the grinding poverty and unjust social systems that cause untold misery for millions, particularly for the poorest of the poor in developing countries. For this reason, it should go without saying that professionals working overseas (or at home, for that matter) should never engage in any activities that smack of corruption, or that—innocent though they may be—give the appearance of corruption.

Giving and accepting bribes is corrupt behavior and, as such, is unethical and illegal. But gift giving is an important ritual in many parts of the world, especially in non-Western countries. Professionals working overseas will undoubtedly be offered small gifts and be invited out to dine. The question then becomes, when does a gift or an evening at a restaurant become a bribe? Is the gift a token of appreciation or an attempt to influence? Should you graciously accept or politely decline? And what about the proverbial "free lunch"? Is it true that there is no such thing? Should you be the one to pick up the tab? Or should you insist that everyone pay their own bill?

Some companies have clear-cut, explicit policies about not giving or accepting gifts, food, or any favors from another stakeholder—not a lunch, not even the smallest token of appreciation. Other companies try to set limits on the type and cost of gifts you are permitted to exchange. For people working for these companies, the guidelines are clear. But for most people working overseas, especially foreign aid workers, the rules are not so clear.

There is no formula for determining the line between a gift and a bribe. It is a judgment call. You need to figure out what constitutes a culturally expected act of courtesy and generosity and what might be meant to influence. The purpose of this chapter is to present some of the social, cultural, and economic factors to consider when making your decision.

The exchange of gifts and food is a culturally accepted ritual that reflects on both the giver and the receiver.

The exchange of gifts and food is a cultural ritual in most of the world—a ritual that demonstrates your respect and appreciation; that reflects your social status, resources, and generosity; and that gives a message about the value you place on the relationship. Exchanging gifts is a way to put a seal on your relationship. Neglecting to behave in a way that is considered to be proper in this regard reflects badly on the individual and even on the family and culture.

This gift-giving ritual takes many forms. For instance, in some European countries, you would never accept a dinner invitation without taking a gift of flowers, wine, or sweets. This is a simple courtesy and a way of expressing appreciation to your hosts. In Asia, the exchange of gifts and meals is an important (and expected) way of showing respect for the receiver and a way for the givers to demonstrate their status and good will.

These gift-giving rituals operate at the institutional level as well. Where a country hosts an international event, the participants are usually treated to an evening of traditional food and music and sent home with small gifts, often gifts with cultural significance. This is standard expected behavior. The more generous the gifts and the more lavish the meal, the more the host gains in status and respect.

Do not underestimate the importance of these gift-giving rituals. Make the effort to find out the cultural norms about gift giving in the country where you are working. To ignore them is to bring shame upon yourself and your organization.

It is considered normal (and expected) to treat a colleague or guest to a meal.

There is no harm in buying a colleague lunch once in a while, in my view. Think about it. In most international settings, you are invited to meetings and other gatherings where meals are served. When you go on field visits, your hosts often provide refreshments. So it is only fair that you reciprocate once in a while when the occasion is right.

One good occasion to buy your local colleagues a meal is when you are traveling together on field visits. For instance, if you are on a field visit and your counterparts do you the favor of taking you to see a special tourist attraction, you can thank them by picking up the tab for lunch. But be sure to tell them in advance that lunch is on you, so they can order what they like without worrying about the cost.

Let people give of the little they have.

It is a terrible thing to always be on the receiving end, to feel like a beggar, constantly dependent on the largesse of someone else. Being an eternal recipient—whether it is a recipient of aid or a recipient of advice—is one of the most soul-crushing aspects of poverty and "underdevelopment." So don't just give to the people you are working with. Let them give to you as well.

You will strengthen the collegial nature of your relationship if you allow your foreign counterparts to give something to you, be it advice, a meal, or a ride home. This normal give-and-take in your relationships shifts the power relationships in the usual donor-recipient dynamics into relationships characterized more by equality and mutuality.

Over the years, my foreign colleagues have helped me in many ways—big and small. One colleague even loaned me one hundred dollars in local currency when I got stuck in a rural area with no cash to my name. He seemed delighted to come to my aid, and in the weeks that followed, he recounted the story of my rescue to all who would listen.

Unfortunately the stories are sometimes more painful than amusing.

I also recall the time when a village midwife caught and killed her only chicken (right in front of my eyes) so that she could serve me a meal, when it was really her family who needed that food. But I knew that there was no way I could refuse. She was not going to be satisfied unless I allowed her to serve me that chicken—a process that took the entire afternoon, by the way.

In many ways, it really is more blessed to give than to receive. All people deserve to experience the joy of giving, however impoverished they are. Let people give to you of what they have, however little.

Let people give to you in their own way.

You can't tell people how to give to you; they have to give to you in their own way.

When I was a microfinance volunteer in a small town in Tanzania, I walked to work. Occasionally I would buy a few mangos or bananas from two friendly little boys who were supplementing their family incomes by selling fruit. Other children I would pass on the road would ask for money, but never these little guys. Slowly I got to know them and, toward the end of our time in the town, another volunteer and I invited them along with us for ice cream and once invited them over to play soccer.

One day I told the boys I would soon be leaving. We exchanged addresses and said our sad good-byes. Then one of the little boys dug into his pocket and pulled out a handful of Tanzanian shillings. With great dignity, he presented the coins to me and said, "Take the bus."

Janet, Development Professional

Don't overdo it.

In most situations you should accept small inexpensive gifts—tokens really—graciously, and you should reciprocate. But you should not encourage frequent gift giving, and should never accept costly items. People could, in fact, be trying to influence you. But even if they are not, it is unethical to allow your counterparts to spend any significant amount of money on you, whether they can afford it or not, and most cannot.

Likewise, just as you don't want your colleagues to spend their limited funds on gifts for you, be careful not to let them spend too much of their

JOURNAL NOTE

Today was the last day of this assignment, and my counterpart was late. When she finally arrived, I found out why. She had been out searching for some crisp new Cambodian bank notes (called riels) to complete my son's foreign money collection. What a surprise! Of course, I reimbursed her for the cash involved, but I can never pay her back for her time and effort. She has a second job teaching English at night because she can't survive on her salary. Her kindness and generosity toward me are very humbling.

Cambodia, 1997

JOURNAL NOTE

Yesterday Adrian and I escaped from the conference for a few hours and went to the waterfront for a drink. He is quite excited about his promotion and thinks he will be able to make a real difference in his new job. But he's had a rough start. One of his first overseas visits was to a development project in a drought-stricken region. When he first arrived, the village chiefs welcomed him with great ceremony and seated him in a place of honor, where he spent the better part of the afternoon listening to speeches in the sweltering heat, all the while wondering how the people managed to survive. Finally the formalities were over and he was invited to eat. But as he looked down at the meager supply of food that was set out and saw the scraggly, pot-bellied children in the crowd, he told his hosts that he wasn't very hungry after all and suggested that they feed the children first. As he put it, "the people were not impressed," and the atmosphere quickly turned sour. He now realizes his mistake. The villagers had offered him what little they had, and he didn't have the graciousness to accept it.

Manila, 1990

personal time touring you around. Some governments and companies arrange tours and shopping trips for foreigners, but this is the exception, in my experience. Generally you shouldn't expect your counterparts to tour you around unless you are convinced that they really want to. Even then, be sure not to take advantage and overdo a good thing.

Don't give more to people than they can give to you.

It's nice to buy little gifts for your counterparts' child or to bring them back a small item from one of your trips, especially if it is something that they cannot purchase locally. But here again be careful not to overdo it. If you give too much, too often, people feel obligated to reciprocate, and many simply can't afford to give you a gift in return.

VOICES FROM THE FIELD
I took a gift of food to a family in Pakistan to thank them for taking the time to let me interview them over several days, only to find that this caused them great embarrassment. They were poor refugees and unable to provide a gift in return.

Dave, Media Representative

One suggestion is to take a photograph of a counterpart's family and give it to them in a simple frame. A photograph of a loved one is a meaningful gift and is always appreciated.

Let your gift giving involve a thoughtful exchange. Don't let it turn into a burdensome obligation.

A FEW NOTES ON CULTURE

Your local colleagues may dress the same as you do, speak the same language, have the same education, and even give the same opinions, but don't assume that they *are* the same. Don't assume that people brought up in another culture look at the world the way you do or that they respond to things the way you would—they may or they may not. The same could be said for every individual you meet, whether in your home country or abroad. But when you add cultural diversity to the mix, a person's perceptions and response to situations becomes even less predictable.

Culture matters. It can be a challenge to "read" a situation in a culture that is foreign to you, and you may sometimes find that you don't fully understand the dynamics of what is happening around you. The following are a few tips to help prepare you for working in a new cultural environment.

Learn about the culture.
Begin by reading about the culture you will be working in. Your knowledge of the country's history, politics, and culture will enrich your overseas experience and will give you the basic knowledge you need to get started. Your advance knowledge of the cultural rules will also help you avoid making embarrassing mistakes.

Avoid stereotyping.

A word of caution here: Learn about the culture of the country, but don't assume that everyone who grew up in that culture has adopted the attitudes and behaviors you have read about. Culture isn't the only factor that shapes human beings. Life circumstances and personality traits are also powerful influences. It is a mistake to make assumptions about any one individual based on what you have read or heard about their culture. There is tremendous diversity within cultures. To really understand the people you are working with, do what you do at home—get to know them as individuals, one person at a time.

Keep checking for clarity.

When you can't read a situation or when you don't know what to do, check with your local colleagues. Start with open-ended questions such as "What is the correct thing to do when we enter the chief's house?" Listen carefully to the answer. If you think you were told that people take off their shoes when they enter the chief's house, you can check that you understood correctly by asking a closed-ended question—one that can be answered "yes" or "no." Back to our example, you might say, "Should I take off my shoes when I enter the chief's house?"

When you are working in a foreign country, keep checking that your understanding of the situation is correct. Otherwise you may never

I had been working in South America when I was transferred to Nepal. I was used to the hugging and open expression of the Latin Americans and thought I was showing my appreciation for the good work my Nepali male secretary did when I gently patted him on the head. Immediately his face turned a bright red and he slid down in his chair. I assumed he just felt embarrassed to be praised in front of his colleagues. It was only some time later, outside the office, that he had the courage to tell me, "Madam, do you remember the day you patted me on the head? In our culture, it is the same as if I patted you on your bottom. Now how would you like that in front of the director?" I apologized profusely and learned not to go around patting people on the head in a Hindu setting.

Theresa, International
Health Professional

know. The people that you are working with may be too polite or too embarrassed to tell you unless you ask.

Try "wasting" a little time.

Time may mean money in Western industrial societies, but in many parts of the world people take a different view of time and may not be willing to do business with you until a personal, trusting relationship has been established. So don't be in too much of a hurry to "get down to business." Relax and go with the flow. Remember that "relationships are everything" in many parts of the world and that "small talk" and other casual interactions with your colleagues are key to relationship building. And, yes, relationships take time.

VOICES FROM THE FIELD

A Pakistani consultant I was working with had a teaching assignment in Indonesia. After lecturing for twenty minutes, he told the students a joke. Nobody laughed. So he asked, "Do you understand what I say?" They are polite to guests, and answered "Yes, sir." So he carried on lecturing, but still there seemed to be no expressions of understanding on their faces and no show of emotion. He thought this a bit strange. After another fifteen minutes or so, he asked again, "Do you understand what I say?" Again they answered, "Yes, sir." Then the consultant asked, "Well, what percentage do you understand?" One of the students stood up and said, "About ten percent, sir."

Theresa, International
Health Professional

Don't be in too much of a hurry to "get straight to the point" either. For example, you may be in a meeting where the discussion seems to be going nowhere, where people are talking in circles. But resist the temptation to intervene. It may be that the parties involved are trying to reach consensus—the name of the game in many cultures—and that the group doesn't want to make a decision until everyone has had their say and until everyone reaches agreement. In this situation, a successful outcome means that everyone is a winner. There are no losers, and no one loses face. This process takes time. Don't try to rush it.

Learn the greeting rituals.

In many cultures, greetings are important rituals that set the stage for

JOURNAL NOTE

This morning I was taking a leisurely hike up a narrow mountain pathway in the Lake Titicaca area when I noticed an Aymara Indian woman behind me, hurrying up the path. As soon as she caught up with me, she slowed down to my pace. There we were, walking shoulder-to-shoulder along the narrow mountain trail. Then she smiled and pointed ahead, as if she were trying to show me something or tell me something, but I couldn't figure out what it was. She seemed to want to pass me, and I couldn't understand why she didn't. Since we didn't know each other's languages, all we could do was smile back and forth. Finally, as I was smiling at her, I happened to nod my head. That was all she needed. She smiled back and hurried on up the trail ahead of me. When I told my colleague about this encounter, he explained that the woman was being polite, asking permission to pass me and go on ahead. When I nodded, she assumed I had given that permission.

Peru, 1980

everything that follows. In these cultures, a person "that didn't even greet" is considered to have behaved very badly. Greetings are exchanges that show interest, care, and respect. Find out about the cultural practices regarding greetings in the country and show your respect by following them, no matter how busy you may be.

Learn the common greetings in the language of the person you are speaking to. I have often been amazed to see how a person's face lights up when I greet them in their language, no matter how bad my pronunciation. Take the time and effort to learn a few words of greeting in the local language, and get your relationships off to a good start.

Take time to enjoy traditional events.

The local people you work with may invite you to participate in their traditional celebrations and will be happy if you agree to join them. But if you do participate, make sure you have the time and energy to get

JOURNAL NOTE

This was a particularly busy Saturday morning. I had a lot of shopping to do. Saturday mornings are the only time that the stores are
open outside of working hours, and I was in a big rush. But every time
I turned around, I ran into one of my local colleagues. In this culture,
I couldn't just wave. I needed to stop and talk. These kind people
would consider it rude and highly inconsiderate to pass me by on
the road without greeting me and showing their interest and concern
by asking about my children, my work, my plans for the weekend,
and anything else that seemed related to my well-being. Of course,
I was expected to do the same. It seemed like everyone I knew was
out shopping. So with all these encounters, I only accomplished half
of what I had intended. But I came home feeling good. I like being a
part of this new community.

Southern Africa, 1984

into the spirit of the day. These community events often start late and
tend to go on and on. If people get the impression that you are simply
"enduring" it all, you will destroy any goodwill you created when you
agreed to join them in the first place. Participate if you can relax and
enjoy it. But if you can't—if you are too tired or too busy—it is best to
stay home.

Avoid a confrontational communication style.

A discussion that seems "open and frank" to you may be considered rude
to people from cultures that avoid direct confrontation. In many cultures
communication is less direct than it is in the Western world, and the way
people express things may seem understated to someone from a Western industrialized society. For example, employees who are performing
poorly may be told that they could do a "little bit" better. Similarly, people from non-Western cultures may not seem to come out and say directly
how they feel. It may seem to Westerners that they are "beating around
the bush" and not saying what they really mean. In some cultures, people

even go through intermediaries to get their message delivered, rather than speaking directly to the person concerned.

Listen carefully to the interactions around you and take note of the way the people you work with communicate with one another. Don't "tell it like it is" in a culture where the communication style is less direct.

Avoid a harsh tone in written communication.

Avoid being too direct in written communication as well. When things are written down in black and white, the message can appear harsh. With written communication there is no opportunity to soften your message and show good will with facial expressions and tone of voice. Your only means of conveying the "spirit" of the message is through the words you put down on paper.

In the Western world, people are encouraged to write direct, simple sentences in the active voice. For example, an acceptable communication would be as follows: "Please complete the enclosed questionnaire as soon as possible and forward it to our office." But in many other parts of the world, the word "please," used in this way, sounds too much like an order. A more acceptable communication style would be softer in approach and might go something like this: "I would be grateful if you would kindly complete the enclosed questionnaire and forward it to our office at your earliest convenience."

Note the tone and style of the written communications you receive from the foreign stakeholders you are working with and make sure that your own written communications don't seem unduly abrupt and harsh in comparison.

Respect your elders.

In traditionally oriented societies, age and experience are highly valued. It is the "wise" respected elder who is held in esteem, not the up-and-coming young executive. Even if these respected elders are not the official decision makers, they can wield a lot of influence. If you can gain their support, your work will be far more likely to succeed.

You can identify those elders that command respect by observing how others interact with them. In meetings, for example, note whom the participants defer to, whom they ask for advice, and whose opinion carries the most weight.

Once you have identified the influential elders, gain their support by treating them with the same respect and deference as do their compatriots. You can demonstrate this respect by consulting with them regularly. Don't present them with a done deal. Explain to them what you are planning to do—step by step—and explain why. Ask them for advice. Above all, listen to what they say.

If you want to succeed in a traditionally oriented society, respect your elders. You may be surprised at how much you can learn from them.

Be prepared for surprises.

When you live and work in another culture, accept that there is always much that you will never know, no matter how hard you try. But don't let this worry you. The people you are working with don't expect you to know all the ins and outs of their culture. Relax and enjoy the surprises. This is what makes working overseas so interesting.

JOURNAL NOTE

My latest lesson about the culture on this island is this: Never tell people how much you like something of theirs. If you do, they will give it to you!

Today I told one of the young officials how much I liked her writing pen. It was decorated with interesting designs and gold trimmings—obviously a gift or a souvenir. Well, lo and behold! as soon as the words were out of my mouth, she insisted on giving it to me. Despite my protests, she wouldn't take "no" for an answer. I feel bad, because the pen was obviously special to her. I had better not tell anyone that I like their clothes—they might take them off and give them to me.

Micronesia, 1993

In the end, it's not much different from home.

Many years ago I conducted an evaluation of a special cross-cultural communications course we were developing for health professionals. We divided the professionals in two groups. One group attended the regular lectures, and the second group attended the regular lectures plus the special class.

At the end of the year, we evaluated the performance of both groups by observing them taking a medical history of a patient from another culture. We were surprised and somewhat dismayed at the results.

We found no difference in the performance of the two groups. The students enrolled in the special class did not perform any better than the students who had only attended the regular lectures. Our special class was not effective in improving cross-cultural communication.

Interestingly, what we found was that the students who performed best were the students who had consistently demonstrated a caring attitude and good communication skills with patients in general. These students gave sensitive care to all people, including those from a culture they didn't understand.

For me, the lesson is this: In the end, working effectively in another culture is not that much different from working effectively with people at home. It is all about respect, sincere caring, and good communication skills.

BRIEFINGS AND DEBRIEFINGS

In many international jobs, particularly short-term jobs, you will brief key stakeholders on your arrival and debrief them on your departure. Generally the stakeholders you brief and debrief will be the senior officials or executives with direct responsibility for the activity you have been hired to implement, such as the head of the department you are working in. So briefings and debriefings present you with a good opportunity to discuss your work with those in leadership positions. The purpose of this chapter is to help you make the most of this opportunity.

Briefings

Like courtesy calls, briefing sessions are scheduled soon after your arrival. But, unlike courtesy calls, the briefing session is a specific discussion of your scope of work with the person in charge. Briefings give you the opportunity to learn firsthand what you are expected to accomplish during your stay. Given the ambiguity in so many overseas assignments, you will want to take advantage of this valuable opportunity to clarify your role.

Every briefing is different. Briefings vary according to many factors, such as the country, the organization, the nature of the job, and (perhaps most of all) the preferences of the stakeholders. Some people who brief you may simply want to meet you and wish you good luck. Others may want an in-depth discussion of your proposed plans. Some will be very directive, telling you exactly how they want you to proceed. Others want you to tell them.

The following are some suggestions for managing these briefings, no matter what form they may take.

SHOW COURTESY AND EXPRESS APPRECIATION.

Briefings aren't courtesy calls, but courteous behavior is a must. A good way to start your meeting is to say how pleased you are to meet the person in charge and to express your appreciation to all who are present (including your counterparts) for the opportunity to discuss your assignment with them. Your polite demeanor and good manners will be appreciated and will get you off to a good start.

USE THE APPROPRIATE TITLE TO ADDRESS THE PERSON YOU ARE BRIEFING.

This is not the time for informal chitchat. Show respect for the position and status of the person you are briefing by addressing them with the proper title, such as Mr., Ms., Professor, Dr., or Minister. People from Western countries sometimes think that calling a person by their first name shows an interest in estab-

VOICES FROM THE FIELD

A representative of our home government aid agency came to the country for the first time to monitor the progress of one of the projects. She had a bright and breezy manner but caused affront when she interviewed a senior government official and called him by his first name. She seemed oblivious to the disrespect she had showed him.

Eleanor, Government/
Church Liaison Officer

lishing a friendly relationship, and it may. But speaking on a first-name basis is entirely inappropriate in this situation. Use the proper title. If you don't know how to address the person you are scheduled to meet, ask your counterparts.

ASK FOR ADVICE AND TAKE IT.

Don't present your work plan as if it is cast in stone. Speak in terms of what you are *proposing* to do and explain why. Then ask for feedback, and listen carefully to what you are told. Show a willingness to take advice and make changes. Seeking advice is another way to show respect for the knowledge and experience of the person in charge.

CLARIFY HOW YOU WILL WORK TOGETHER.
Some leaders may want you reporting back to them on a regular basis. Others will only want to meet with you upon completion of your assignment. It is important to clarify this. You will also want to know which decisions require consultation and which you can make in collaboration with your counterparts. The briefing session is an opportunity to find out—right from the beginning—how best to manage these working relationships.

Debriefings

Debriefings at the end of your assignment provide the opportunity to present your work and make recommendations to high-level decision makers. As was the case with briefing sessions, debriefings come in many forms. Some are one-on-one meetings with the person in charge, often with your counterparts present as well. Other debriefing sessions are more like formal meetings, with all the stakeholders present. The following are some general guidelines to keep in mind, whatever form the debriefings may take.

EXPRESS APPRECIATION FOR THE SUPPORT YOU HAVE RECEIVED.
Acknowledge the support and guidance you have received from the organizations involved and from the people you have worked with, particularly your counterparts. Give some specific examples. You don't have to lay it on, but speak with sincerity and let your local colleagues know how much you enjoyed working with them and how much you yourself have benefited.

LET YOUR COUNTERPARTS TAKE THE LEAD.
It is often more effective and more acceptable to have your local

counterparts give the presentation and take the lead in the discussions, but this may not be possible. The counterpart may not want this role because he or she lacks the skills or the confidence or both, and the leadership may not be satisfied unless they hear directly from you. You need to read each situation as it presents itself. Sometimes the opinion of the outside expert carries special weight, sometimes not. Discuss this with your counterparts. Whatever the decision, your local counterparts will appreciate that you gave them the option to take the lead.

DISTRIBUTE A BRIEF SUMMARY REPORT.

At the time of your debriefing, provide a one- or two-page bullet-point summary of your outputs, findings, and recommendations. This written summary will help you focus your presentation on the main points and make it easy for people to follow you, particularly if you are speaking in a language other than their mother tongue.

There is often considerable lag time between the time your final report is written and the time it is released to the field. This is because many such reports are not released until they are reviewed, edited, and "cleared" at many levels. So another reason your foreign colleagues will benefit from having a written summary is that this report can serve as an interim working document until the final report is released.

STAY IN YOUR PLACE.

As you present your findings and recommendations, avoid being prescriptive. You are the resource person, not the decision maker. Your role at the debriefing session is to report on your activities and outputs and to provide the responsible authorities with quality information and expert advice. The decisions are up to them. Effective international workers and advisers know their place and stay there.

END WITH A MESSAGE OF HOPE.

No matter how challenging your assignment has been, let your final words of this assignment be words of encouragement. Focus on the positive. Remind people of what has been accomplished thus far, often under the most difficult circumstances. If you end your assignment with a message of hope, your counterparts will leave your debriefing session with the confidence that they can continue to move forward, no matter how difficult the road ahead.

MAKING A DIFFERENCE

Professionals who accept overseas assignments expect to make a difference—to bring about change. And they do. The very presence of an outside foreigner brings about change and affects the organizations and individuals. So if you accept a position in a foreign country, whether a short-term job or a long-term assignment, don't worry. You *will* make a difference. The question is: What kind of a difference will you make? How much of a difference? How lasting a difference?

The difference you make will depend in part on how you approach your international job and on how you interact with your local colleagues. The purpose of this chapter is to discuss some of the ways you can make a difference for the good, a difference that really matters.

Build a broad base of support.

Collaborate with all relevant stakeholders and seek their support. Don't let yourself get identified with a certain group of enthusiastic supporters to the exclusion of others. You could wake up one morning to find your key supporter transferred to another department and replaced by the official you ignored. Involve as many people as possible in your work so it will be sustained when you are gone.

Bring positive energy to your work.

You can make a difference with a positive "can do" attitude. You don't need to go over the top with your enthusiasm. That would only irritate your local colleagues and give the impression that you don't understand or fully appreciate the difficulties they face. But don't go on and on about what's wrong either. Most people already know what's wrong—probably much better than you do—and have likely been struggling with these problems for years. If everything had been going well, they wouldn't have needed to recruit you. Don't add to the doom and gloom. Rather, bring positive energy and enthusiasm to the task at hand, and give people hope that progress can be made.

Focus on the key priority areas for action.

You won't be able to tackle everything that you think needs doing or changing, at least not all at once, no matter what your job description says. Don't allow yourself to get bogged down with side issues. Decide on the few things that really matter and work toward those.

Keep it simple.

Don't make things more complicated than they need to be. Find ways to make it easy for people to implement the changes you are recommending. For example, if a simple spreadsheet will do, don't overwhelm people with your fancy data-entry system. Introduce user-friendly systems that will work for people.

Be sensitive when giving feedback.

In some international jobs, you will be reviewing proposals—funding and otherwise—from local counterparts and members of the community. People often put heart and soul into those proposals, and negative comments can cause hurt and resent-

I like to allow for "overnight inspirations" after meetings and workshops. The work is often intense, and ideas and information are flowing rapidly. A little time for reflection helps me more fully consider the questions and gain greater insight into the issues.

Patti, Development Professional

ment. Give critical feedback in a helpful way. Rather than saying that a section of the proposal is unclear or otherwise inadequate, explain how the section could be "strengthened" by doing such and such. Even better, give an example and help draft something. Give feedback in a way that the recipient sees as supportive rather than critical.

Be efficient and timely where money is involved.

If your job involves the funding of local activities, be clear about the date the funds will be available and make the payments on time. This is particularly important for international aid organizations funding projects and providing relief commodities. Don't put the local people in the position of having to call your office over and over again to inquire about the money they have been promised. This will cause resentment and destroy whatever good will has been established. Distribute funds on time. Don't make people beg for money.

Encourage local decision making.

In the ideal world of international consulting, the local stakeholders would be involved in decision making at every level. They would give input, and the final decisions would then be made on the basis of consensus. The international worker would not be expected to "sell" one particular strategy but would serve as a resource person and facilitator.

But we do not work in an ideal world, and many job contracts specify the strategy you are expected to implement as well as the results you are expected to deliver. Sometimes the decision makers have been consulted, but not the implementers on the ground. Sometimes not even the decision makers have been properly consulted. If you find yourself boxed into such a situation, you can make a difference by identifying those decisions, big and small, that still remain to be made—and there will be many—and by encouraging your local colleagues to make those decisions. Take every opportunity to put the decision making back into the hands of the local people.

Be prepared *for* change and be prepared *to* change.

The one thing you can count on in your international assignment is that there will be changes—changes in the government, changes in your job, changes in your counterparts, even changes in yourself. Some of these changes will be the result of your work. But most will have nothing to do with you, and the reason for many changes may forever remain a mystery to you.

VOICES FROM THE FIELD

I applied for a job at a medical institute in a developing country. The interviewers included the recruiter from the international placement agency and local representatives from the institute itself. The local representative asked if I would be willing to make changes in the educational approaches of the medical institute. I answered that I would be very willing to assess the situation but that I would discuss my findings with the local faculty so that they—not I—could decide on the changes. The interviewer from the placement agency said that I must not have understood the question, since it was intended to determine whether or not I was competent as a change agent. I replied that I fully understood the question and stood by my answer. I got the job! The representatives from the developing country wanted to have control over when and how changes might be made and knew better than to hire someone who would hand out advice prematurely.

Sandra, International Health and AIDS Adviser

Whatever the reason, these changes will bring opportunities as well as challenges. Write your action plan in pencil and make the most of the opportunities that change brings your way.

If it doesn't happen, let it go.

Sometimes things just don't work out—no matter how well thought out your plans, no matter how much local support you think you have, no matter how hard you try. If, despite all your efforts, the planned activity just never gets off the ground, it is time to step back and take stock. Something is going wrong. Maybe the stakeholders only said yes to your plan because they didn't want to offend you. Maybe your plan conflicts with activities being proposed by another worker. Maybe there are political undercurrents that make implementation of your plan difficult. There are many such maybes, and it can be difficult to figure out exactly where the problem lies. If you find that your plan just isn't happening, let it go for a while. Accept that when you work in a foreign country, there are many things you may never know, many factors operating that you do not understand. Back off and revisit the situation later, when you have a better idea what is going on.

Have a long-term vision, but make every day count.

You, like most professionals working abroad, will want to make a difference in the long term—a difference that will be sustained over time. You don't want everything you have worked on to fall apart when you leave. You have a long-term vision of the difference your work will make. You can help ensure the sustainability of your work by building broad-based support for your work and strengthening the capacity of your counterparts. But this may not be enough to ensure that your work survives you.

The external funding for your activities may end with your departure, and the resources for your project may simply dry up. The counterparts you have worked with may change jobs. A new administration may call a halt to the activities you have initiated. Many things can happen. So, while you have a long-term vision, make every day count. Accept the possibility that what you do today may be "it." The workshop you conducted may never be repeated. The program you started may end. But this does not mean that your work is not sustainable.

Your project may not be sustainable, but the work you have done on a day-to-day basis may indeed be lasting, in ways you may never know. So make the most of each day you are in the country. Avoid wasting your time on things that are just "for show," such as writing a report no one wants to read. Do the things that matter, even if they only seem to matter today. Keep your long-term vision. Work toward sustainability. But make a difference one day at a time.

Prepare a report someone *will* want to read.

You will have to prepare a report at the end of your assignment. Your report is an important product of your assignment, so make it a report that will make a difference. Be clear about who you are writing for and why, and write clearly, simply, and to the point. The longer it is, the less likely it will be read.

VOICES FROM THE FIELD
My students conducted applied research in rural communities and produced valuable information relevant to the development of the communities they studied. They wanted to publish their reports, so we started a journal. The journal lasted as long as the consultant facilitated the process. When she left the country, it died. Though it was not sustainable, copies of the journal were used for many years as guides for conducting community-based research.

Sandra, International Health and AIDS Adviser

Begin your report with an introduction that clarifies the purpose of your report and the intended reader. Is the purpose of your report to demonstrate to your employer that you met the objectives of your assignment? Is the purpose to make recommendations to the foreign government? Is the purpose to provide guidance for your counterparts? Make the report you write a product that the intended reader needs, wants, and can understand.

Describe your activities and findings, but be careful not to toot your own horn too much. Acknowledge the accomplishments and contributions of others, including local officials and colleagues, referring to their positions, not their individual names. The specific names of the persons who contributed to the content of the report can be listed in the annexes. Also include a list of the documents you used in preparing your report. Whatever you do, don't give the impression that you think nothing happened before you arrived on the scene.

Every experienced international professional will have at least one tale

JOURNAL NOTE

This conference has been a wonderful, affirming experience. My presentation went well, but, best of all, I ran into one of the students I had taught in Africa over twenty year ago. She is now a senior official in her government ministry. She asked me, "Do you remember that workshop you conducted after our group had graduated?" I certainly did remember that workshop. Everything had gone wrong, and I had spent my time chasing presenters that hadn't shown up and making sure there was toilet paper in the bathrooms. I'll never forget it. Of course, all I said was, "Yes, I do remember." Then she looked at me and said, "It was that workshop that made me realize I could do more, I could be more."

Barcelona, 2002

to tell about consultants who "parachute in," take up everyone's time asking questions and photocopying their reports, compile it all, put their name on it, and fly away. Job done. This type of report may have its value, but only if the contributions of all the stakeholders and informants are properly acknowledged.

Make recommendations that have some hope of being implemented. You will not be taken seriously if you recommend the impossible. When you make a recommendation, explain your reasons and give practical information and guidance on "next steps." Don't fill your report with too many "shoulds." Address the long-term vision, but focus your report on the priority areas for immediate action, on the concrete actions that will move things forward.

Government offices around the world are full of job reports stacked up on shelves, gathering dust. Don't let your report be added to the pile. Take the time to write a report that will make a difference—a readable report that will help people make wise decisions, a report that will encourage people to sustain the work that has begun, a report that will inspire them to accomplish even more.

You will make a difference, but you won't change the world.

You *will* make a difference when you work in a foreign country, but you may not make as much of a difference as you had hoped. This is not reason for despair. Some of the challenges you will face are so complex, so deep rooted, and so intertwined with the social and political environment that a "quick fix" simply isn't in the cards. You can't address all the issues—certainly not as a foreigner—but don't despair. You can do *something.* You can make a difference by making a humble contribution. Do not expect to do more than that. International workers who start out thinking they can change the world often end up discouraged, bitter, and cynical. Don't let this happen to you. Give it your all and do what you can. Your modest contribution will make a difference, often in ways you will never know.

Let the country make a difference in you.

You will make a difference in the country you work in, and the country will make an even bigger difference in you. Whether you intend it or not, working abroad will change you forever. Never again will you see the world in quite the same way. If, as the old adage goes, "travel broadens your horizons," then working overseas will broaden your perspective even more. After an overseas assignment, you may find that your values have shifted, that you are not quite so sure of long-held opinions, that you are not quite so convinced of the rightness of your decisions. You may find that some things you held dear don't seem to matter so much anymore and that some things you once took for granted suddenly take on greater importance. Let it happen. Personal growth is one of the benefits of working overseas. Yes, you will make a difference when you work in a foreign country, and the biggest difference may be the difference you allow to happen inside yourself.

PROFILE OF THE EFFECTIVE INTERNATIONAL WORKER

This is my checklist. This is the person I want to hire for an overseas job. These are the qualities I am looking for when I am recruiting international workers.

▶ TECHNICALLY COMPETENT
The bottom line: has the required qualifications, knowledge, and experience

▶ ADAPTABLE
Able to apply their knowledge to the new country situation
Does not start the assignment with a set formula for action
Does not import solutions from other countries
Does not constantly talk about how "we did this in X country"

▶ KNOWS THE PRIORITIES
Knows what really matters and focuses on that
Lets the nonessentials go

▶ SKILLED IN THE ART OF CONSULTING
Communicates effectively

Builds productive relationships with all stakeholders
Seeks advice more often than gives it
Not compelled to tell everyone everything they know

▶ PERSONALLY COMPETENT
Able to function effectively in a foreign environment
Has good manners and common sense
Does not expect the organization or its counterparts to take care of them
Can manage without a personal assistant or secretary
Does not take themself too seriously

▶ RESPECTFUL OF THE CULTURE
Follows cultural rules regarding appropriate dress and social behavior

▶ SUPPORTIVE OF THEIR LOCAL COUNTERPARTS
Promotes their counterparts, not themselves
Does not take advantage of counterparts' hospitality and generosity
Sensitive to the realities of their colleagues' living and working situations

▶ HAS A POSITIVE "CAN DO" ATTITUDE
Looks for the good and builds on that
Recognizes the challenges but doesn't constantly dwell on "what's wrong"

▶ KNOWS HOW TO WORK WITH GOVERNMENTS
Knows the protocols (and asks when not sure)
Shows respect for government officials
Follows government regulations and secures the required permissions

▶ WILLING TO BE JUST PLAIN HELPFUL
Steps in and helps as needed—adding paper to the fax machine, photocopying a report, giving a counterpart a lift—doing the little things that make life easier for the local counterparts

The indefinable more . . .

In addition to the characteristics and skills listed above, there are other things I am looking for when I hire an international worker—qualities that are difficult to define but that make all the difference to their success. I am talking about integrity, wisdom, and caring, qualities that you can recognize when you experience them, when you feel them, but that don't quite fit on the checklist.

In my international work, I have encountered people who seem to do everything "right," everything I am recommending in this book, but somehow it doesn't come off. It just doesn't seem sincere. These people know what they should do, but their words and actions appear rehearsed, as if they are applying a formula. It's just not them.

I was working for a large international NGO on a strategic planning exercise when our work was "interrupted" by a fierce battle between the two prime ministers in a leadership crisis in Cambodia—bullets flying, people fleeing the city, memories of Pol Pot times. We were all hunkered down for three days, trying to survive while the war raged. When the shelling stopped, we cautiously started back to work. I was floored when no one even mentioned what we had just gone through. So I took a deep breath, stopped the meeting, acknowledged how terrified we all were, and spoke to the need to give ourselves some space to recover from these experiences and to be realistic about what we could accomplish under these circumstances.

Patti, Development Professional

When you are working abroad, your greatest tool is yourself—your sincerity, your caring, your wisdom, and your sensitivity. In the end, being successful on a job overseas depends as much on who you are as it does on what you do.

A FEW LAST WORDS

Care, But Take Care—Don't Let It Break Your Heart

Some of you reading this book will be working with international aid organizations or with church missions, providing relief and development support for desperately poor people living in appalling conditions. The stress you experience when faced with such needs can be overwhelming, especially when you are in day-to-day contact with people who are suffering right before your eyes. But even international aid workers whose offices are far from the front lines of despair are under great pressure to deliver help to those in need. Add this pressure to the stress of change that most expatriates working overseas experience, whatever their job (the stress of change, the stress of a new job, the stress of being away from family and friends) and you have a mix that can literally make you ill.

If you are working under such difficult circumstances, you need to take care of yourself. Get into a routine that includes eating healthy food at least twice a day, exercising, and sleeping a reasonable number of hours. Spend time with your family. At the very least, try to avoid overworking day in and day out over a long period of time. The cumulative stress that results from excessive workloads takes a heavy toll on your outlook as well as on your health.

Don't let your experiences isolate you. Many people working under desperate circumstances feel that back home "there is no one who knows and no one who cares" what they are going through. But it is important to share your story with someone, to try to find at least one person who is interested and stay in regular communication with him or her. You will need this person when you return to your home country. You will need someone who understands what you have lived through, someone who understands the culture shock you may experience when you return home, someone you can talk to if you are feeling depressed. Stay in touch with your other friends and family members at home as well. Even if you don't think that they care about your work, chances are that they care about *you*, probably very much. You will need that network of support when you return home.

In order to stay positive when working in a desperate situation, be realistic about what you can accomplish. Accept that you can only make a humble contribution and recognize that your contribution, however limited, has value. If you expect too much of yourself, you risk losing your effectiveness. If you descend into a downward spiral of exhaustion and despair, you risk becoming so pessimistic that you start questioning whether you are doing any good at all. Worst of all, you may even stop caring. Don't let yourself get to this point.

You can't save the world, but you can make a difference in someone's life, and helping even one person will help *you*, will give you hope to carry on. There are many opportunities to do something concrete for a person in need. Sponsor the education of a promising student. Help a single mother to start a small business. One colleague, who was besieged every day by street children, sponsored a feeding program at the neighborhood church. He probably didn't change their lives, but he did *something*, and the *something* he did to meet the immediate needs of the children he encountered every day energized *him* and gave a personal meaning to the work he was doing to address the root causes of their suffering.

But, try as you may, there may come a time that you just can't face another day of the misery around you. When that day comes, it is time to take a break. You will know that you are getting to that point when you find yourself feeling hopeless, when you start becoming unreasonably critical of your colleagues and sarcastic about your work. If that day comes, it is time for a break. It is time to start taking care of you.

As an international worker, your greatest tool is yourself. Take care of yourself so that you can continue to care for others.

INDEX